The Science of Bullying

CRAFTED BY SKRIUWER

Copyright © 2024 by Skriuwer.

All rights reserved. No part of this book may be used or reproduced in any form whatsoever without written permission except in the case of brief quotations in critical articles or reviews.

For more information, contact : **kontakt@skriuwer.com** (www.skriuwer.com)

TABLE OF CONTENTS

CHAPTER 1: UNDERSTANDING BULLYING: AN INTRODUCTION

- *A clear definition of bullying and why it matters*
- *Key elements that define bullying (imbalance of power, repetition, harm)*
- *Common reasons for bullying behaviors*
- *Impacts on targets, bullies, and bystanders*
- *A look at how bullying can grow in different environments*

CHAPTER 2: SOCIAL FACTORS THAT LEAD TO BULLYING

- *Peer pressure and the desire for popularity*
- *Social hierarchies and group behavior*
- *Cultural norms and values that influence aggression*
- *Family influences on children's actions*
- *Ways to address and reduce social triggers*

CHAPTER 3: EMOTIONAL COMPONENTS OF BULLYING

- *How anger, sadness, and fear fuel bullying*
- *Common emotional experiences of targets*
- *Hidden reasons that drive someone to bully*
- *The role of empathy in reducing harmful actions*
- *Helping both targets and bullies manage strong emotions*

CHAPTER 4: PHYSICAL & VERBAL FORMS OF BULLYING

- *Examples of physical harm and the damage it causes*
- *Verbal teasing, name-calling, and threats*
- *Signs of physical and verbal bullying*
- *Addressing incidents quickly and consistently*
- *Offering support for targets and guidance for those who bully*

CHAPTER 5: CYBERBULLYING & ONLINE HARASSMENT

- Why bullying online can feel nonstop
- Common types of cyberbullying, from harassing messages to doxxing
- Strategies for reporting abuse and staying safe
- Role of parents, schools, and platforms in stopping digital harm
- Helping targets regain confidence

CHAPTER 6: PSYCHOLOGICAL EFFECTS ON TARGETS

- Short- and long-term impacts on mental well-being
- Challenges with self-worth, anxiety, and depression
- Warning signs parents and teachers should watch for
- Supporting emotional healing and resilience
- Preventing further harm through open communication

CHAPTER 7: LONG-TERM CONSEQUENCES FOR THOSE WHO BULLY

- Academic struggles and legal risks
- Difficulty forming healthy friendships and relationships
- Emotional costs, including guilt and shame
- Potential issues with authority and workplaces
- Guiding them toward change and positive behavior

CHAPTER 8: SCHOOL ENVIRONMENTS AND BULLYING

- Creating a culture of respect and clear rules
- Teacher training and supervision strategies
- The importance of open communication and reporting
- Involving parents and guardians in solutions
- Building supportive climates that discourage meanness

CHAPTER 9: FAMILY DYNAMICS AND PREVENTION

- How home life shapes behavior toward peers
- Detecting and stopping sibling bullying
- Building empathy and open communication at home
- Balancing love, boundaries, and discipline
- When to seek outside help and professional advice

CHAPTER 10: COMMUNITY INVOLVEMENT AND INTERVENTION

- Bullying in parks, youth centers, and neighborhoods
- Role of community leaders and local law enforcement
- Partnerships between schools, families, and community programs
- Spreading consistent anti-bullying messages outside of school
- Creating spaces where children feel safe and included

CHAPTER 11: THE ROLE OF EMPATHY

- Why understanding others' feelings reduces cruelty
- Empathy skills that prevent mean behavior
- Helping the target feel heard and supported
- Bystander actions rooted in compassion
- Bringing empathy into daily classroom and home routines

CHAPTER 12: BUILDING SELF-WORTH AND RESILIENCE

- The link between low self-esteem and bullying
- Activities that boost confidence and coping skills
- Resilience as a shield for targets and a deterrent for bullies
- Encouraging a healthy sense of identity
- How family and school can foster stronger self-belief

CHAPTER 13: HANDLING CONFLICT AND ANGER

- Recognizing early signs of tension and frustration
- Teaching children to name and manage intense feelings
- De-escalating arguments before they become bullying
- Healthy conflict resolution steps and tools
- When to seek extra guidance for anger issues

CHAPTER 14: CHANGING GROUP BEHAVIOR

- How group dynamics can encourage or discourage bullying
- Roles of leaders, bystanders, and social norms
- Gaining support for positive changes from classmates
- Handling cliques and exclusion patterns
- Uniting the whole group around empathy and respect

CHAPTER 15: LEGAL AND POLICY PERSPECTIVES

- Why laws and school policies matter in curbing bullying
- Defining bullying and setting consequences in official rules
- Cyberbullying and legal accountability
- How parents and schools can use policies effectively
- Balancing discipline with education and understanding

CHAPTER 16: ADDRESSING BULLYING AT HOME

- Detecting if your child is bullying or being bullied
- Sibling rivalries vs. true bullying
- Supporting a bullied child with open talks and resources
- Guiding a bully to better behavior and remorse
- Monitoring online interactions within the family

CHAPTER 17: RESTORATIVE STRATEGIES

- Focus on healing and rebuilding damaged relationships
- Restorative circles, mediation, and apologies
- Benefits for both the target and the person who bullied
- Training facilitators to keep sessions safe and fair
- Combining restorative methods with other interventions

CHAPTER 18: EMPOWERING BYSTANDERS

- How onlookers can shape the outcome of a bullying incident
- Overcoming fear and uncertainty to help
- Practical ways to stand up, distract, or report
- Providing encouragement and protection for brave bystanders
- Creating a culture that supports speaking out

CHAPTER 19: MODELS AND PRACTICES THAT HELP

- Overview of proven school-wide approaches
- Social and Emotional Learning, peer mediation, and structured programs
- Parent and community involvement in broad initiatives
- Tracking progress and adapting methods over time
- Building a consistent message against bullying

CHAPTER 20: SUPPORTING POSITIVE RELATIONSHIPS

- *How strong connections safeguard against bullying*
- *Creating emotional safety at home and in friendships*
- *Team-building in schools and peer support groups*
- *Respecting differences and valuing each person's strengths*
- *Moving forward with empathy and understanding for lasting change*

Chapter 1: Understanding Bullying: An Introduction

Bullying is a repeated act of harm or intimidation directed at someone who may not be able to defend themselves easily. It is a serious problem that can happen anywhere people spend time together. It can happen in schools, playgrounds, online spaces, or even at home. When someone is bullied, they often feel scared, anxious, or sad. The person doing the bullying might use words or actions to show power or control over someone else. This can involve making threats, calling names, spreading rumors, or even hurting someone physically. In many cases, bullying is not a simple conflict or disagreement. Instead, it involves a clear pattern where one side has more power or influence, and that side uses it in a hurtful way.

Many people think of bullying as a normal part of growing up. They might say that it is common for children to tease or fight with each other. However, bullying goes far beyond a small tease or a playful argument. It causes real harm to the target, whether that harm is emotional, social, or physical. Over time, repeated bullying can damage someone's self-esteem and sense of safety. It can also make them feel alone, as if nobody cares about them or wants to help them. This is why understanding the basics of bullying is important. Only by knowing what it is and how it works can we learn ways to address it.

One of the key elements of bullying is the imbalance of power. This can come from being bigger, older, more popular, or even from having certain social connections. For example, some children might be liked by many classmates and use that social support to pick on someone who does not have as many friends. When they decide to make fun of a certain person, others may follow along, which can make the person being bullied feel outnumbered and helpless. In other cases, the power imbalance might be related to family position, such as an older sibling bullying a younger one. Sometimes, it can also involve differences in wealth, ability, or other factors.

Another feature of bullying is its repeated nature. A single event of teasing or a one-time argument, while still hurtful, does not always qualify as bullying. Bullying usually happens again and again over a period of time. This repetition adds to the distress of the target. Each day, they might worry about what will happen next. The fear of the next comment, joke, or action makes them feel trapped. This cycle can have a big impact on how someone sees themselves and how they manage their day-to-day life.

There are many reasons why a person might bully someone else. Sometimes, they may have learned these behaviors from adults or peers in their lives. If a child grows up seeing family members handle problems with aggression, they might believe that this is the normal way to interact with others. In other cases, a child might bully others as a way to fit in or get attention. They might think that by putting someone else down, they can appear cool or strong. They might also bully others to get what they want, such as money, homework answers, or control of certain spaces. Regardless of the reason, bullying causes harm to the target. It may also cause social and emotional problems for the bully in the long run.

Bullying can take many forms. It can include physical harm, such as pushing, kicking, or hitting. It can also include verbal harm, such as calling someone names, making fun of them, or threatening to hurt them. Emotional bullying might involve leaving someone out on purpose, spreading rumors, or embarrassing them in front of others. In the modern age, bullying often continues online, which is sometimes called cyberbullying. Through social media, text messages, or email, some people post cruel comments, share private information, or send mean messages. All these forms can have serious consequences, but they share a common thread: they hurt someone over time and make them feel unsafe or upset.

Targets of bullying often feel shame, fear, and sadness. They might blame themselves for what is happening and wonder if they have done something wrong. They might feel worried about going to school or other places where the bullying occurs. Over time, these feelings can affect how they see themselves. They might stop wanting to do hobbies or activities they once enjoyed. They might also avoid social events or friendships because they fear being teased or hurt again. In some cases, children who are bullied experience problems such as trouble sleeping, headaches, or stomachaches that are linked to stress. Grades may also suffer if the child is worried, depressed, or too distracted by fear during class.

Those who bully others might also have problems or conflicts in their own lives. They could be dealing with stress or anger. They might have difficulties at home or in school. In many cases, they do not know healthier ways to handle strong feelings or conflicts. They may try to manage their pain or fear by causing pain to someone else. Others might do it to seem popular or powerful, hoping that their classmates will follow along. Even though they appear strong, many bullies struggle with hidden issues like low self-esteem or confusion about how to behave. Their bullying behavior might get them attention for a short time, but it can hurt their relationships and their emotional growth in the long run.

It is also important to look at the role of bystanders. These are people who see bullying or know it is happening, but they are neither the main bully nor the target. Bystanders can play a big role in stopping bullying or letting it continue. If bystanders laugh along, join in, or stay silent, it might send a message that bullying is acceptable. This is because the bully sees that no one is standing up against them. On the other hand, if bystanders speak up, tell a trusted adult, or offer support to the target, they can help cut off the bully's social power. Bystanders who stand up for the target can change the situation, even if they are not close friends with the target or the bully.

There are many negative effects of bullying on everyone involved. The target might develop low self-worth, anxiety, or depression if the bullying continues for a long time. They may also find it hard to trust others or make friends in the future. Those who bully might develop unhealthy ways to deal with anger or frustration. They can miss the chance to learn how to cooperate, share, and show kindness. If their bullying continues, they could face trouble in school, legal problems, or broken relationships later in life. Bystanders who do nothing might feel guilty or upset, and they might come to believe that they are also powerless in difficult situations.

Many schools, families, and communities have started to pay more attention to bullying. People see that it can cause lasting damage. As a result, they are taking steps to teach kindness and respect. They are also exploring ways to address the needs of those who bully, so they learn better ways to handle their feelings or problems. However, bullying is still a big issue, and it does not disappear just by setting rules or handing out punishments. Understanding what bullying is, why it happens, and how it affects everyone is the first step toward real change. We need to keep looking at the roots of bullying behaviors, the environments that allow them to grow, and the best methods to prevent or reduce them.

In this book, we will go deep into the different factors that lead to bullying, as well as its emotional, social, and long-term effects on both targets and those who engage in it. We will explore how bullying takes shape in different places, including online spaces, schools, and communities. We will also talk about the legal points that can affect how bullying is handled. There will be discussions on the value of empathy, family involvement, and community support. We will also look at strategies that can reduce bullying, such as helping bystanders become strong helpers rather than silent watchers.

It is also crucial to point out that bullying is not something that happens because of one cause. It often arises from a mixture of personal, social, and cultural factors. For example, a child might have a hard time controlling their anger because they feel stressed at home. At the same time, their friends might cheer them on when they act mean. Or, there might be a school culture that does not punish bullying strictly, so the bully believes they can get away with it. All these pieces can come together, creating a problem that is difficult to solve.

The consequences of bullying can extend far beyond a single moment in time. Children who are bullied in elementary school might still feel the emotional effects in high school. They might worry that people will tease them again, or they might develop habits like staying quiet in class to avoid being noticed. Meanwhile, children who bully might never learn proper ways to handle their emotions, which can hurt them when they have to deal with challenges later in life. This is why early detection and prevention efforts can be very helpful. When we spot bullying signs sooner, we have a chance to redirect the behavior of the bully and help the target feel safe.

Society's view of bullying has shifted over the years. In the past, people sometimes brushed it off, saying, "Kids will be kids." Yet, research has shown that the harm of bullying is real. It can affect mental and physical health. In addition, technology has given bullying new forms, such as cyberbullying, which allows people to harass others even from a distance. This can make the bullying feel nonstop, since it might follow the target to their phone or computer. Understanding these changes is part of what makes it important to study bullying from many angles, so we can figure out how to reduce it and help those affected.

As we go through each chapter, we will look at different types of bullying, why they happen, and how they shape people's lives. We will also talk about solutions and ideas that can be used in schools, communities, and homes. By learning these details, we can support targets of bullying and guide those who bully toward better behavior. We can also encourage bystanders to speak up. The goal is to lower harmful actions and build safer places for everyone. But it all begins with understanding: recognizing that bullying is a serious problem, seeing how it works, and realizing that each of us can do something to help stop it.

Children, teenagers, and adults can all be targets or witnesses of bullying. Even though this might seem like a problem only among children, bullying behaviors can appear at any age. A boss might bully an employee by threatening them or insulting them in front of colleagues. A neighbor might bully another neighbor by shouting at them or starting rumors. Learning about these aspects can help us see that bullying is not only a problem for children. It is a broader issue that can affect many parts of life. Still, focusing on children and schools is crucial, because that is where we can shape positive habits that last into adulthood.

We must also remember that not all children who act mean are bullies in the strict sense. Sometimes, children have disagreements or fights without one side trying to keep power over the other. This is why it is important to distinguish between normal conflict and bullying. In a normal conflict, both sides can have equal power or be upset over something that can be settled. In bullying, one person has or tries to get more power by targeting someone who is less able to defend themselves. That difference is key to identifying real bullying. By making this distinction, adults can respond better, giving extra support to those who face real intimidation and repeated harm.

Lastly, it is good to keep in mind that bullying is preventable. With the right steps, care, and knowledge, communities can become safer. Schools can teach respect and have policies in place to handle bullying cases. Parents can speak with their children about how to treat others with kindness. Children can learn that it is better to cooperate and speak up rather than pick on someone. People who bully can be taught new ways to manage anger and stress. By working together, we can reduce bullying and help children grow up in an environment where they feel safe and supported.

This first chapter has aimed to show the basics of what bullying is and why it matters. It is more than just teasing; it is a harmful act with effects that can last for a long time. Bullying affects the target, the bully, and everyone who sees it. Stopping bullying begins with knowledge: knowing what it looks like and why it occurs. In the chapters ahead, we will look at these issues in more detail. We will explore the social, emotional, and psychological parts of bullying. We will also talk about strategies that can lead to better outcomes for everyone involved.

Chapter 2: Social Factors That Lead to Bullying

Bullying does not happen in a vacuum. It often involves social factors that shape how people interact with each other. These factors can include peer pressure, family influences, school climate, and the broader culture. When we talk about social factors, we mean all the forces in a group or community that affect how people behave or treat each other. Learning about these factors helps us see why bullying can grow in certain places and what we can do to address it. If we look closely at peer relationships, norms, and expectations, we can find clues about how and why bullying starts.

One of the strongest social factors that can lead to bullying is peer pressure. Peer pressure happens when people feel pushed to act in a certain way so that they can fit in with a friend group or social circle. This can be positive if friends encourage each other to work hard in school or help others. But it can be negative if friends or classmates push someone to act mean. For example, if a popular child starts teasing another child, some classmates might join in because they do not want to stand out. They might laugh at unkind jokes to avoid being singled out themselves. This can create a chain effect where more and more people take part in bullying. In these situations, many bystanders do nothing or even side with the bully because they fear losing their own social standing.

The desire to be accepted is strong, especially for children and teenagers. During these years, friendships can feel like the most important thing in the world. Young people want to be liked, and they might do almost anything to keep their place in a peer group. If that group encourages teasing or name-calling, a child might do it, even if they know it is wrong. This does not mean the child is heartless or cruel by nature. It might mean they are worried about being laughed at or excluded if they do not join in. Peer pressure can be subtle or direct, but it often shapes behavior in powerful ways.

Social status is another factor that can lead to bullying. In many schools or youth groups, some children stand out as leaders, while others have less influence. Those with higher social status might use bullying to keep their position. They might want to prove they are the ones in charge, so they single out someone who seems weaker or less popular. Or they might show off in front of their friends by putting someone else down. This can make them feel more confident or look more powerful to others, even though it is at the expense of someone else's well-being. These social hierarchies can be found in many settings, and they are often linked with bullying.

Sometimes, a group of friends forms around someone who is seen as powerful, and they start to copy that person's mean behavior. They might all gang up on someone they perceive as an outsider or who does not share the same interests. In other cases, the one with social power might not even need to do anything directly. Their friends might bully someone just to please the leader or get their attention. This dynamic can make it very hard for the target to find a safe space, especially if the bullying group is large or influential in the school.

Cultural norms can also play a role in bullying. For example, if a culture teaches that aggression is a normal way to solve disagreements, children might see bullying as an acceptable action. If a community places a high value on competition and winning at all costs, some children might decide that bullying is okay if it helps them stay on top. Cultural norms can also shape who is targeted. Sometimes, people from certain ethnic backgrounds, religions, or communities are more likely to be bullied if the culture around them supports negative stereotypes. Other children might be bullied because of their appearance, such as their weight, clothing style, or any physical differences, if the wider culture places strong emphasis on looking a certain way.

Family dynamics can also add to the social environment that leads to bullying. Children often learn from what they see at home. If they see family members yelling or using threats to handle conflict, they might think that is how they should behave with peers. If parents do not talk about kindness or respect, children might not realize how important those values are. In some homes, children might be under a lot of pressure to be perfect or strong. This can lead them to release their stress on someone else at school. Or they might bully others as a way to feel better about themselves if they do not meet certain family expectations. All these family influences can shape how children behave in social settings.

School climate is another major factor. The term "school climate" means the overall feel or culture within a school. Do teachers treat students fairly and kindly? Do students feel safe expressing themselves? Are there clear rules about bullying, and do adults enforce them? If the school climate is harsh or unfair, bullying may be more common. For instance, if teachers or other staff ignore unkind behavior or blame targets for "being too sensitive," students might believe bullying is acceptable. On the other hand, if the school makes it clear that bullying is not allowed and encourages students to speak up, there may be less bullying. The school climate can also be affected by how much support or training teachers get on handling bullying. If adults do not know how to spot or address it, bullying can grow unnoticed.

Social media and online platforms can also influence bullying. Online environments sometimes encourage people to say things they would never say in person. The internet can make it feel like there are no real-life consequences. A comment or post can go viral quickly, drawing in many people to join in. This can happen on social networks, in games, or through group chats. The result can be a form of bullying that seems unstoppable, because it can follow someone anywhere they have an internet connection. If a person gains social approval by posting mean comments about someone, they may keep doing it. This online crowd effect can boost the mean behavior and give the bully more power.

Another social factor is the presence of "cliques" or small groups that exclude others. When a group decides who is "in" and who is "out," they might use bullying to maintain that line. For instance, a clique might spread rumors about someone or make fun of them to ensure they stay on the outside. The members of the clique might feel closer to each other by sharing a common enemy. This sense of unity can be very appealing to some children, leading them to take part in bullying so they can remain accepted by their group.

Gender expectations can also shape bullying behavior. Sometimes, boys might feel pressure to act tough, so they use aggression against peers. Girls might be expected to be "nice," yet bullying can take more hidden forms in female groups, like exclusion, rumors, or name-calling. These patterns can be connected to larger social ideas about how boys and girls are supposed to behave. When a child goes against these ideas, they may be bullied for not fitting in. It is important to note that these patterns are not fixed. Still, they offer insight into how social pressures and expectations can add to bullying problems.

Teachers, counselors, and parents can help by paying attention to these social factors. For example, if they notice that a group of students follows a certain leader, they can encourage positive leadership that includes everyone. They might ask that leader to guide a team project where everyone's ideas matter. Adults can also help children learn how to handle peer pressure. They might organize small group lessons on saying no to mean behavior or standing up for classmates. If adults do not address the social factors, children might think it is normal to tease or hurt others. So, a proactive approach can stop bullying from taking root.

It is also important for schools and community organizations to create an environment where kindness and respect are seen as positives. This can include praising children who show helpful or thoughtful actions. It can also involve forming clubs or activities that bring different types of students together. When children get to know peers who are different from them, they might be less likely to bully those peers. They might realize that each person has strengths and that differences can be interesting rather than bad. As a result, the social divide that fuels bullying can shrink.

Parents have a big part to play, too. They can set a good example at home by treating others with kindness. They can talk to their children about the impact of words and actions. They can teach them to handle anger in ways that do not hurt others. They can also ask about what is going on at school. Open communication is key because children might not talk about bullying unless they are asked. If a parent finds out their child is bullying someone, they can look into the reasons behind this behavior rather than ignoring it. Then, they can guide the child to better methods of handling problems or frustrations. If a parent finds out their child is being bullied, they can work with teachers or counselors to address it. By being proactive, families can help reduce bullying at its roots.

Communities can get involved by creating youth programs that promote respect and cooperation. For example, sports teams can be a place to learn fair play, but only if coaches make sure bullying or teasing does not become part of the team's culture. Mentorship programs can pair older students with younger ones, helping build friendships and support. Neighborhood groups can hold events that bring families and children together, so they can get to know one another outside of school. When people form real connections, there is less reason to target each other.

Some children who bully might not have strong social skills. They might not know how to make friends or keep them. They might turn to bullying as a way to get attention or feel important. This is why teaching social skills can be a strong preventive measure. Schools and youth programs can run lessons on how to communicate needs, handle disagreements, and control strong emotions. Children can learn to see that they can build a sense of worth by helping others and working together, rather than by pushing others down. Once children have healthier ways to form friendships and manage problems, they are less likely to bully.

It is also worth noting that bullying sometimes happens when there is a lack of adult supervision or involvement. In some schools or neighborhoods, there may not be enough adults watching the halls, playgrounds, or online chats. Without guidance, children might feel free to bully others or may not see it as something that adults take seriously. If schools or communities hire more staff or train volunteers to watch and help children during activities, they can catch and address bullying behaviors early. Sometimes, just knowing that someone cares and is ready to step in can make children think twice about bullying.

Role models in media and entertainment can also affect how children think about bullying. If children see movies, shows, or online videos where a strong character always uses force or mean language to get what they want, they might believe that is normal behavior. Parents and educators can help by talking about what children watch. They can point out that real life is different from fiction. They can discuss how meanness can hurt others deeply. By doing this, adults help children question negative examples instead of just copying them.

In summary, social factors can push individuals toward bullying or keep them stuck in that behavior. Factors like peer pressure, the desire for popularity, family influences, and cultural expectations can work together to shape how children and teens treat each other. When we pay attention to these factors, we can see that bullying is not simply a problem with a single person. Instead, it often grows out of a group dynamic that encourages or ignores unkind actions. By changing the group's attitude and norms, we can create an environment that does not support bullying.

Adults can make a difference by teaching children to stand up for themselves and others. They can explain how to resist peer pressure and how to show kindness even when friends might be acting otherwise. Teachers can establish clear rules about bullying and enforce them. Parents can show what respectful communication looks like at home. Community leaders can create programs where children learn to respect differences and build friendships across various backgrounds.

Each step can make a positive difference in reducing bullying. If a child sees that a teacher, coach, or parent consistently stands against bullying, they might feel brave enough to speak up when they see someone else being teased. If they see that kindness is praised and that bullies face consequences, they might decide not to bully in the first place. Also, if children are taught empathy skills, such as trying to understand how others feel, they might think twice before making someone the target of unkind words or actions.

Addressing these social factors will help us look at bullying from a wide lens. It is not just about the bully and the target. It is about how the entire group responds, the messages that parents and teachers send, and the norms that guide behavior. The deeper we look at these elements, the clearer it becomes that stopping bullying is a shared task. It is a shared responsibility between all parts of a child's life: home, school, online spaces, and community. By working on these areas, we can begin to reduce bullying and create places where respect and kindness stand out more than meanness.

In the next chapters, we will explore more dimensions of bullying, including emotional components and other forms it can take. By understanding all the pieces, from internal emotions to the social scene, we can find better ways to stop these harmful actions from happening. This approach will help everyone—targets, those who engage in bullying, and bystanders—move toward healthier, safer relationships.

Chapter 3: Emotional Components of Bullying

Emotions play a big part in many bullying situations. When we look closely at the feelings on all sides, we can learn a lot about why bullying happens and why it keeps going. Emotions can be complicated, especially during childhood and the teenage years. During these times, people often struggle to understand their own feelings, as well as the feelings of others. This confusion can lead to unkind behaviors if there is no proper guidance. In this chapter, we will examine the emotional side of bullying, including common feelings that targets experience, what drives those who bully to behave as they do, and how these feelings can affect everyone involved.

---

1. Emotions Experienced by Targets

When someone is bullied, they can feel many different emotions. One common feeling is fear. Targets might worry about the next time they will be teased or harmed. This fear can become so strong that the person being bullied avoids places like classrooms, playgrounds, or online spaces. They might think that if they hide or stay silent, they can avoid more harm. Fear can also lead to anxiety, which might show up as shaky hands, sweating, or an uneasy feeling in the stomach. Over time, anxiety can become a serious problem that affects how a person thinks, sleeps, and behaves.

Another emotion many targets feel is sadness. It can be very hurtful to be called names or to be pushed around, especially if it happens again and again. Sadness might come from feeling alone, believing that no one else understands or cares. This sadness can make some people cry easily or seem withdrawn. In other situations, a target may hide their sadness, smiling on the outside but feeling terrible on the inside. If sadness continues for a long period, it might turn into depression, a condition where a person feels hopeless or numb.

Shame is also common. When someone is bullied, they might blame themselves, thinking they caused the mistreatment. This is especially true if the bully or others say it is the target's fault. Shame can make people feel as if something is wrong with them. They might think they do not deserve friends or kindness. Over time, shame can damage how a person sees themselves. They might become too hard on themselves, believing they are not good enough or that they cannot do anything right.

Targets can also experience anger. Being hurt repeatedly can build up a sense of bitterness or rage. Some people who are bullied might lash out at home or become hostile toward their own friends or siblings. Others may keep the anger bottled up inside. While anger is not the same as bullying, it can push someone to act in ways they normally would not. If the anger is never addressed, it can become destructive or lead to more difficulties in personal relationships.

Another important emotion is confusion. Targets might not understand why they are being picked on. They might ask themselves questions like, "Did I do something wrong?" or "Why do they hate me?" This confusion can make people feel uncertain about who they are and how they should act. When confusion mixes with fear and sadness, it can leave someone feeling very lost. This can keep them from seeking help because they might believe that nobody can solve their problems or that the bullying is somehow normal.

---

2. Emotional Drivers for Those Who Bully

While targets often feel sadness, fear, and shame, the person who bullies might have a different set of emotional experiences. One possible driver is a sense of power. Some people bully because it makes them feel strong or in control. They might feel proud when they see the target cringe or run away. This sense of power can be tempting, especially if the person who bullies feels powerless or uncertain in other areas of life. By picking on someone else, they get a quick boost of self-esteem.

However, power is not the only feeling that might push someone to bully. Feelings of anger can also play a role. Some children or teens might face stress or aggression in their own lives. They might have fights at home or feel overwhelmed by personal problems. Without healthy ways to manage these strong emotions, they may displace their anger onto a classmate or neighbor. This does not excuse their behavior, but it can show how intense feelings can lead to harmful choices when they are not guided properly.

Jealousy is another emotion that might drive bullying. A child might envy another classmate's success, looks, or friendships. This jealousy can turn into mean actions or words. They might pick on that classmate to feel better about themselves. The unkind behavior can give them a momentary sense of relief from their jealousy. But it creates a cycle of negativity, because the bully never learns a better way to handle envy or grow their own self-confidence.

Some people bully because they do not feel empathy toward others. Empathy is the ability to understand and share the feelings of someone else. When someone lacks empathy, they might see hurting others as no big deal. They might ignore the target's pain or see it as amusing. This absence of empathy can come from many places: it might be that they have never learned to recognize other people's emotions, or they might have been exposed to harsh behavior in their environment, so they do not realize how deeply words or actions can hurt. The lack of empathy can also tie into a desire to fit in with a certain group that values aggression.

Fear of rejection or vulnerability might also cause someone to bully others first. A child who is worried about being teased for their clothes or background might try to pick on someone else before anyone notices their own insecurities. This behavior can be a way to "protect" themselves by pointing attention toward another person. Over time, this can become a habit, leading them to believe that bullying keeps them safe from being mocked.

3. How Emotions Keep Bullying Going

Emotions can keep bullying going long after the initial incident. For instance, a target who feels fear may not speak up. This allows the person who bullies to continue their actions without facing consequences. The person who bullies might then feel confident or untouchable, which reinforces their mean behavior. Meanwhile, if bystanders see the target remain silent, they might assume the target does not need help, or they might stay quiet to protect themselves.

At the same time, the person who bullies might feel pressured to keep up their behavior for social reasons. If their friends praise them for being tough, they may keep bullying to hold onto that image. This is where emotional reinforcement can come from peers who laugh at rude jokes or encourage mean actions. The cycle continues until someone steps in or until other emotions—like guilt—cause the person who bullies to stop.

4. Emotional Impact on Bystanders

Bystanders are the people who see or hear about bullying but are not directly involved as the main bully or the main target. They can also experience a range of emotions. One of these is fear: a bystander might worry about becoming the next target if they speak up. They might also feel confused, not knowing how to respond. Some bystanders feel guilt after seeing someone get bullied because they wish they had done more to help.

Peer pressure can make these emotions stronger. If the bully is popular, bystanders might worry that standing against that person will cost them their social standing. They might feel torn between doing the right thing and fitting in with their group. These mixed emotions can be stressful. Over time, if bystanders keep quiet, they can carry feelings of shame or regret for not helping. This emotional weight can make it even harder for them to come forward in the future.

5. Recognizing Emotional Warning Signs

Children and adults who notice certain warning signs can step in early to prevent bullying or to give support. For example, if a child seems unusually anxious about going to school or riding the bus, it might mean they fear a bully. If they cry often without a clear reason, it could be due to sadness from bullying. Abrupt changes in mood or behavior can also be an indicator. Maybe a child who used to be happy and outgoing becomes quiet and withdrawn. Or perhaps a usually easygoing child starts yelling at siblings or friends. These emotional warning signs could mean something is wrong.

On the other side, if a child suddenly acts out in mean ways or shows a drop in empathy for others, it might be a sign that they are starting to bully or that they are imitating behavior they have seen somewhere else. They might test boundaries, seeing how far they can go before an adult corrects them. Recognizing these signs early can allow teachers or parents to step in and address the issues before they escalate.

6. Ways to Manage Emotions in Bullying Situations

Learning to manage emotions is essential for everyone involved. Targets can benefit from talking about how they feel with a trusted adult, such as a parent, teacher, or counselor. Sharing fear and sadness can provide some relief and help the child see that they are not alone. Counselors or supportive friends can also teach coping skills like deep breathing, writing in a journal, or practicing a calming hobby. These strategies might not stop the bullying right away, but they can help the target handle stress and feel better about themselves.

Those who bully can also learn healthier ways to manage their anger or jealousy. They might meet with a counselor who can teach them to recognize their triggers. For instance, if they bully more when they are stressed at home, they can learn to talk about their feelings or find safe outlets for stress, like sports or art. This guidance is not about excusing their behavior; it is about giving them the tools they need to change. Once they see that kindness and cooperation can also bring them respect, they might begin to change their actions.

Bystanders can work on handling the fear and anxiety that come from witnessing bullying. They can learn methods to speak up safely, such as seeking help from an adult or offering quiet support to the target. Some bystanders may gather a few friends to stand together against the bully. Having a group can lower their fear of being singled out. Over time, this can lead to a more supportive atmosphere among students.

---

7. The Role of Self-Esteem

A person's sense of self-esteem can be a major force in bullying situations. For targets, bullying can lower their self-esteem, making them feel weak or unworthy. For those who bully, the act might be a way to momentarily boost self-esteem if they feel insecure in other parts of their life. Building healthy self-esteem can prevent both sides of bullying from taking root. When children and teens feel comfortable in who they are, they are less likely to pick on someone else to feel strong. They are also more likely to stand up for themselves if someone tries to bully them.

Schools and families can help improve self-esteem by praising efforts, not just outcomes. For example, a parent might say, "I'm proud of how hard you worked on that math project," instead of only praising an A grade. Teachers can give roles to students that let them explore their strengths, such as leading a class discussion or helping a peer with a problem. This helps children see their own value. It also teaches them to see the value in others, which is a key step toward reducing bullying.

8. Handling Emotional Pain After Bullying Ends

Even after bullying stops, the emotional wounds can last. Some people might continue to feel sad or worried for months or years. They might struggle to trust others or to make friends. This can affect their schoolwork, social activities, and sense of happiness. If someone has been bullied for a long time, they might need extra support to move past the emotional harm. Counselors, psychologists, or trusted adults can help them work through memories of being bullied and learn new ways to see themselves.

People who once bullied others might also need guidance to handle guilt or shame. Realizing that they caused pain can be tough. Some might try to hide from that guilt by ignoring it. However, facing it can help them grow. They might choose to apologize or to do acts of kindness. This can help them let go of their past actions and move forward in a healthier way. Without this emotional work, they could slip back into old patterns if they face stress or difficult emotions again.

9. Creating Safe Spaces to Share Feelings

Safe spaces can help children process feelings related to bullying. These might be school clubs led by a teacher who understands how to manage group conversations about problems and solutions. They might also be support groups where students can share personal stories of being bullied or seeing bullying happen. The key is that these spaces must be free of judgment, allowing everyone to speak honestly. In such settings, children can discover that they are not alone, and they might learn ways to cope by hearing what others have done.

Parents can also set aside time at home to talk about feelings. A daily check-in, such as talking during dinner or before bed, can help a child open up about what is bothering them. If they are upset or stressed, they know there is a regular time and place to share these emotions. This steady routine can help them feel safer and more supported. It can also give parents or caregivers a better chance to spot signs of bullying or changes in the child's mood.

---

10. Encouraging Kindness and Empathy

A strong way to address the emotional components of bullying is by teaching kindness and empathy. When children learn to consider others' feelings, they are less likely to pick on their classmates. They might also notice when someone seems upset or lonely and offer help. Schools can teach simple exercises, like having students talk about how they feel in certain scenarios or how they think someone else might feel. Parents can talk to their children about how words and actions can make others feel. This encouragement of empathy can weaken the emotional basis for bullying, which often relies on ignoring or denying the target's feelings.

It might also help for classes or families to read books about kindness or to watch shows that show caring behavior. While this does not solve everything, seeing examples of empathy in action can spark conversations. For instance, after reading a story where a character helps a friend, children can discuss what might have happened if the character had stayed silent. These discussions build emotional awareness, guiding children to notice and respect feelings.

---

11. The Importance of Emotional Guidance from Adults

Adults—whether they are parents, teachers, coaches, or neighbors—can do a lot to shape how children handle emotions. When adults manage stress and anger in respectful ways, they show children that big feelings can be handled without hurting others. If adults yell or use unkind words at home or in the classroom, children might copy that behavior. On the other hand, if adults apologize when they make mistakes and listen when children talk about feelings, they are setting a positive example.

Consistency matters, too. If a parent punishes a child for a small outburst but ignores a bigger problem like bullying, the child can become confused or feel that no one really pays attention to their deeper emotions. Keeping a fair and caring approach helps children see that adults are there to guide them, not just punish them. If a child does bully someone, the adult can calmly discuss how their actions might have felt to the other person. This approach can help the child understand the emotional cost of bullying without feeling like they are being attacked.

---

12. Building Emotional Skills Through Creative Outlets

Creative outlets can be helpful for children who are dealing with strong emotions tied to bullying. Activities such as drawing, painting, writing stories, or making music allow them to express themselves in ways that might be easier than talking. Through art, a child can show what they are feeling or how they see the world. If an adult sees repeated themes of sadness or anger in a child's drawings, it can be a sign that the child needs help. Likewise, a bully might find a healthier way to channel their emotions by writing or playing an instrument, rather than taking them out on someone else.

Sports and teamwork can also teach emotional balance. In a friendly sports environment, children learn cooperation, patience, and how to handle wins and losses. They see that everyone on the team is valuable. This can lower the need to feel powerful by bullying. Over time, the emotional lessons learned through sports can help a child avoid mean behavior and build empathy for others who are struggling or learning new skills.

---

13. Stopping Emotional Harm Before It Starts

Prevention is always better than trying to fix problems later. If teachers and parents teach emotional awareness early, children will be less likely to resort to bullying. Emotional awareness means understanding how we feel and why. It also includes recognizing how our actions might affect someone else's feelings. Even simple activities like group discussions on feelings can make a difference. Children can learn how to say, "I feel upset when you do that," instead of lashing out or using mean words.

Furthermore, recognizing warning signs of bullying behaviors can allow adults to step in before things get worse. If a child starts putting others down or laughing at someone's misfortune, an adult can have a private talk with them. They can ask, "Why did you feel the need to laugh at that?" or "How would you feel if someone said that about you?" These questions prompt the child to look inside themselves. If done calmly and without shame, such talks can steer the child toward more thoughtful choices.

---

14. Moving Forward with Emotional Awareness

Emotions are central to human life. They color how we see the world and how we treat each other. In bullying, emotions can either fuel the problem or help solve it. By learning about fear, sadness, anger, power, jealousy, and other feelings, we can better understand the problem of bullying. Then we can take concrete steps to handle these feelings in healthy ways. This benefits everyone: the target, who gains coping skills and support; the person who bullies, who can learn to redirect harmful urges; and bystanders, who learn to act with courage and compassion.

When adults make emotional lessons part of everyday life, children grow up with a stronger sense of empathy. They learn that while we cannot always control how we feel, we can control how we act on those feelings. They also see that emotions are not something to fear or hide from, but something to understand and handle wisely. This knowledge can help prevent bullying from taking hold in the first place.

Finally, it is important to remember that each individual is different. Some children might be more sensitive, while others might hide their emotions. Some might need more personal support, while others can adapt quickly. Being open to these differences is key. By focusing on healthy emotional growth, we give children tools to handle challenges, treat others with respect, and seek help when they need it. Understanding emotions does not cure bullying alone, but it forms a solid base for building better relationships and safer places for everyone.

Chapter 4: Physical and Verbal Forms of Bullying

Bullying can appear in many forms, but two of the most common are physical and verbal. Physical bullying involves hurting someone's body or possessions. Verbal bullying involves using words in a harsh or harmful way. Both forms can cause serious harm to the target's well-being. In this chapter, we will examine the nature of physical and verbal bullying, how to recognize them, and how they affect everyone involved. We will also discuss ways to address these forms of bullying so that both targets and bystanders can respond quickly and effectively.

---

1. What Is Physical Bullying?

Physical bullying is when someone intentionally uses their body or an object to harm another person. This can include pushing, hitting, kicking, tripping, or even spitting. Sometimes, it might involve destroying or taking away someone's belongings. For example, a bully might throw a target's backpack in the trash or break their phone. Physical bullying is often the form most people think of when they hear the word "bullying," because the signs are easier to see. Bruises, cuts, or torn clothes can be clear indicators.

Physical bullying does not always happen in isolated places like empty hallways. It can occur in front of others on the playground or in the cafeteria, where many people can see it. In some cases, the bully might want an audience. They might feel a sense of power or excitement knowing that other children are watching. For the target, being harmed in front of classmates can add shame and embarrassment to their physical pain. They may feel humiliated and worry that everyone is talking about the incident afterward.

---

2. Why Does Physical Bullying Happen?

Children or teens who engage in physical bullying may feel a need to prove their strength or dominance. They might feel that hitting or pushing another person is the quickest way to look tough. In some groups, there is a belief that physical fights are a normal part of settling problems. This idea can come from family traditions, media, or social norms where physical aggression is viewed as acceptable. Some young people learn that using force is how you get what you want. Without correction, they continue this behavior at school or in other places.

Another reason physical bullying happens is a lack of impulse control. Some children struggle to think before they act. They might feel sudden anger and lash out by shoving or punching someone. They might also do it if they find something funny, such as tripping a classmate for a laugh. These actions can cause real harm, even if the bully claims it was just a prank. Over time, repeated physical harm can create a climate of fear in a school or community setting. Younger children, especially, can become anxious about moving around hallways or playgrounds if they expect to be pushed or hit.

---

3. Effects of Physical Bullying on the Target

Physical bullying can leave more than just bruises on the body. It can also cause emotional harm. Targets might start to feel unsafe wherever they go. They might worry that someone will push or hit them again, causing them to avoid social settings or even skip school. Over time, this fear can grow into anxiety or panic whenever they see certain classmates or walk through certain areas. The target might also have a hard time focusing on schoolwork because they are constantly on guard.

In addition, the physical pain can lead to ongoing stress. If the bullying is frequent, the target might be in a constant state of worry about the next event. This stress can affect their sleep, causing nightmares or insomnia. It can also affect their health in other ways, such as headaches or stomachaches tied to anxiety. Emotionally, the shame of being pushed around in front of peers can linger. They may feel weak or embarrassed, believing that they cannot defend themselves. This can damage their self-esteem and make them pull away from friends or family members.

---

4. Recognizing Physical Bullying

Children and adults can watch for several signs that point to physical bullying. A child might often have unexplained bruises or cuts. They might try to hide these injuries or make excuses like, "I fell down the stairs," even if the excuse does not match the injury. If they frequently lose personal items such as books, clothes, or electronics, or if those items are often damaged, it might be because a bully is taking or breaking them.

Another sign is if the child starts avoiding places like the school gym, a certain hallway, or a playground. They might say they do not want to go outside during recess or that they dislike a particular activity. This could be because that is where the physical bullying usually occurs. Watching for these signs can help adults spot when something is wrong so they can step in more quickly.

---

5. Addressing Physical Bullying

Physical bullying should never be ignored. Adults can set up clear rules that make it clear that hitting, pushing, or any kind of physical harm is not allowed. These rules must come with consistent consequences so that children see that harmful actions are taken seriously. Teachers, coaches, and other staff should be trained to spot incidents, even if they happen fast. Supervising hallways, cafeterias, and playgrounds is important. If a child feels that adults are paying attention, they might feel safer. The bully might also be less likely to try something when they know they are being watched.

When an incident happens, it is important for an adult to step in right away. They can separate the bully and target, make sure no one is hurt, and calmly talk to everyone involved. The adult can ask bystanders what happened, gather the facts, and speak with the children. If the bully did harm someone, there should be a clear response. This might include removing the bully from the area, talking to them about why their actions were wrong, and contacting parents. In some severe cases, the school or community might involve law enforcement. The goal is to show that physical violence has real consequences and will not be overlooked.

---

6. What Is Verbal Bullying?

Verbal bullying involves words that harm or hurt another person. This might include name-calling, insults, mocking, threats, or hurtful jokes. Like physical bullying, verbal bullying can happen anywhere—on the bus, in the classroom, in the lunch line, or even online if it uses spoken or written words in a harmful way. While it does not leave bruises or cuts, the damage can be just as serious, because words can make someone feel ashamed or scared. Verbal bullying can also include making comments about someone's appearance, weight, or background, as well as using slurs or hateful language.

One reason verbal bullying can be so hard to stop is that it often happens quickly. A student might whisper a mean comment under their breath, or they might say something cruel as they walk by. Another challenge is that some people do not see words as harmful as physical actions. They might say, "I was just joking," or, "It was just words." However, repeated unkind words can hurt a person's self-confidence and sense of safety.

---

7. Why Does Verbal Bullying Happen?

Verbal bullying can happen for many of the same reasons as physical bullying. The bully might want power or attention. They might feel the need to impress their friends, or they might take out their anger on someone else. Sometimes, people find it easier to say mean things than to act them out physically. They might think it is less risky or that they can escape punishment by saying they were joking. However, the words can still have a lasting effect on the person they target.

Some children might engage in verbal bullying because they see adults or older siblings talk to others in a rude or hateful way. If a child grows up hearing family members insult each other, they might believe it is normal to speak that way. In other cases, children hear unkind language in movies or online and then copy it at school. They may not realize how hurtful it really is, or they might not care as long as it makes them seem tough.

---

8. Effects of Verbal Bullying on the Target

Words can create wounds that do not show on the outside. When someone hears repeated insults, they might begin to believe the mean things said about them. If they are called "stupid" every day, they might stop trying in school because they think they cannot learn. If they are mocked about their looks, they might become anxious about how they dress or appear to others. Over time, this can reduce their self-esteem. The damage from verbal bullying can affect a person's choices and behavior for a long time, even after the bullying stops.

Targets of verbal bullying may also feel humiliated if the comments are made in front of other people. They might replay the insulting words in their minds over and over, feeling shame or anger. Some children might pretend they do not care, but inside, they might be deeply hurt. This pain can lead to sadness, embarrassment, or depression. In some cases, the person who is bullied might begin avoiding social events or trying to stay invisible, hoping the bully will ignore them. They might miss out on forming new friendships or pursuing hobbies they enjoy.

---

9. Recognizing Verbal Bullying

Verbal bullying can be harder to catch than physical bullying because it leaves no obvious marks. However, there are clues. A child might talk about the mean names they are called at school, or they might appear upset after a certain class or lunch period. Some children might start to avoid speaking in class for fear they will be teased if they say something wrong. Others might show changes in mood or behavior, such as crying after reading a note passed around by classmates.

Sometimes, adults might only see the aftermath—for instance, the target crying in the restroom or a friend comforting them. It takes time and attention to find out what caused the tears. If the child says they were teased, that is a sign that verbal bullying could be going on. Paying attention to sudden negative shifts in a child's self-esteem or willingness to participate can also point to verbal bullying.

---

10. Addressing Verbal Bullying

Like physical bullying, verbal bullying needs a prompt response. Adults can clearly define what language and behaviors are not acceptable. They can explain that using words to harm someone is just as serious as using fists. Teachers can create a supportive atmosphere where respectful conversation is encouraged. They might have class discussions about the power of words and how name-calling or gossip can hurt people's feelings. If students know the school takes verbal bullying seriously, they may be less likely to do it or more likely to report it.

When an incident of verbal bullying is reported, an adult should talk calmly with those involved. They can ask the bully why they said those words and explain how those words can cause harm. The adult can also make it clear that saying, "I was just joking," is not an excuse. If the bully continues this behavior, there should be consequences, such as losing privileges or receiving a written warning. For severe or repeated cases, the school might call parents in for a meeting. The main goal is not just to punish, but to stop the hurtful behavior and help the child see why it is wrong.

---

11. Supporting Targets of Physical and Verbal Bullying

Targets need support to feel safe again. They need to know that someone is on their side. This support can come from parents, teachers, counselors, or friends. Talking about what happened can help them release bottled-up feelings. They might share how they felt when they were hit or insulted, and how that fear or shame has affected their life. By talking, they can also learn that they are not alone. Adults can reassure them that bullying is never their fault and that they deserve respect.

In addition, children might need practical help, like having an adult walk with them in hallways or watching carefully during break times. Friends can also help by sticking together. When a child has even one supportive friend by their side, they often feel braver and less isolated. This can stop bullies from targeting them, because many bullies look for someone who is alone or who has no one to back them up. Schools might also offer counseling sessions or group activities that help children build self-esteem and learn problem-solving skills.

---

12. Encouraging Bystanders to Help

When it comes to physical and verbal bullying, bystanders can make a real difference. If a bully sees that no one supports their actions, they might stop. Bystanders do not have to directly confront a bully if they feel unsafe. They can help by quickly getting an adult or by calmly asking the target to leave the area with them. Even giving a kind word or a quick check-in with the target after the event can help them feel less alone.

Schools can teach bystanders to speak up in a safe way. Students might practice phrases like, "That isn't okay," or "Please stop." They can also learn to text or call a teacher if they see bullying happening. By practicing these responses ahead of time, students feel more prepared to step in. These small actions can protect targets and let the bully see that their words or actions are not admired.

---

13. Moving Past Physical and Verbal Bullying

Stopping physical and verbal bullying is a goal that schools, parents, and communities can work toward. It starts with clear rules, consistent consequences, and strong support for targets. But it also requires deeper changes in how people communicate. Children should learn that hurting others, whether with their hands or their words, is not a normal way to solve problems. They should see positive examples of how to talk about frustrations or differences without causing harm.

If a child has developed a habit of using words or physical force to get what they want, they might need extra help to change. This could be one-on-one guidance with a counselor or another caring adult. They might practice conflict resolution skills, like explaining their feelings calmly or offering a compromise. They might also learn stress management techniques so they do not lash out in anger. With consistent help, many children can learn to shift from bullying behaviors to respectful ones.

---

14. Healing After Physical and Verbal Bullying

Once the bullying stops, the process of healing begins for targets. They may need time to rebuild trust in their surroundings and in their peers. If they have been physically harmed, they might still feel soreness or pain, or they might need medical care. Emotionally, the healing could involve recognizing that they are not weak or worthless just because someone hurt them. Their view of themselves might need a boost through counseling, family talks, or supportive friendships.

The person who carried out the bullying might also go through a form of healing. They could feel guilt for what they did. They might feel anxiety if they fear punishment or loss of friendships. Sometimes, realizing the damage they caused can be a turning point, motivating them to make amends and change. They might apologize or offer to help the target in some way, though this depends on the situation. Not all bullies are ready to acknowledge their actions, but having caring adults around can make it easier for them to move in a healthier direction.

---

15. Working Together for Safe Environments

Physical and verbal bullying create harm at both personal and group levels. Children who face these forms of bullying might struggle with schoolwork, friendships, and their own sense of self. Classmates who witness it might feel uneasy or upset. This can affect the entire school atmosphere. Yet, by working together, adults and children can reduce these harms. Schools can have clear anti-bullying policies, so everyone knows the rules and the results of breaking them. Teachers can offer open communication, encouraging students to talk about issues and get help without fear of blame.

Communities can also play a role. Neighborhood groups, youth centers, or sports clubs can build awareness by discussing how to handle bullying. They can set the tone that no physical or verbal harm is allowed. Older teens can be mentors, guiding younger kids toward kinder ways of interacting. Parents can share stories and solutions with each other, so they do not feel alone if their child is bullied or is bullying others. The wider the circle of support, the more likely it is that children will feel safe and learn better ways to handle conflicts.

---

16. Hope for Change

It can be discouraging to see physical and verbal bullying persist in schools and communities. But progress is possible. Many programs around the world have led to declines in bullying by teaching children to handle disagreements respectfully and to speak up for each other. Families and teachers who maintain open dialogue can catch problems early. Kids themselves can learn to be kinder, more aware of differences, and more willing to support someone in need.

When children realize that hitting or insulting someone is never the best option, they can shift toward healthier communication. This builds stronger friendships and a more positive environment for everyone. While no place is perfect, consistent effort and understanding can cut down on bullying. With the right support and education, children can grow into adults who choose respect over harm.

By knowing how physical and verbal bullying work, we are better equipped to handle them. We can step in when we see them happen, offer help to those who need it, and guide those who are causing harm to find a better path. Each time people stand against bullying, they reinforce a message that kindness is stronger than cruelty. That is a message children can carry with them as they grow, making their communities safer and more caring places for all.

By working to remove physical and verbal bullying from our schools, neighborhoods, and online spaces, we create a kinder society. Nobody should have to live in fear of being kicked, shoved, or insulted. Everyone deserves the chance to learn, grow, and connect with others without being hurt. When adults and children unite to stop these forms of bullying, real change can happen, and everyone can feel a little more secure in their daily lives.

Chapter 5: Cyberbullying and Online Harassment

The internet has brought many benefits to our world. People can connect with friends far away, learn new things at any time, and find communities of people with similar interests. While these are good changes, the online world can also be a place where bullying happens in different ways than we see in person. When bullying moves onto phones, apps, or websites, it is often called cyberbullying or online harassment. This can involve cruel messages, threats, rumors, or embarrassing posts shared for many people to see. In this chapter, we will explore what cyberbullying looks like, why it can feel so overwhelming to targets, and how families and schools can work together to limit the damage.

What Makes Cyberbullying Different?
Cyberbullying shares many features with other forms of bullying. It involves repeated acts meant to harm or scare a target. The bully might want attention, power, or a sense of control over someone else. However, cyberbullying has some features that make it different:

It can happen around the clock. In-person bullying usually happens at school, in the neighborhood, or during events. Once the target goes home, they might find peace from bullying for a while. But cyberbullying can reach them at any hour through messages or social media. Targets might receive mean comments or see embarrassing posts late at night, making them feel like they have nowhere to hide.

It can spread very fast. One harsh post or photo can be shared, forwarded, or copied many times in a short amount of time. This can make the target feel overwhelmed because many people might see the hurtful content. Even if the bully removes the post later, it could still have been saved or shared by other users.

It can be anonymous. Some online platforms allow people to hide their real names. This can give a bully the sense that they can act without consequences. They might create fake profiles or accounts to say unkind things. For a target, it can be scary not knowing who is behind the messages or posts.

It can be more public. While physical or verbal bullying might happen in front of a few people, online content can be seen by an entire friend list or even the public. This larger audience adds to the stress and shame that a target may feel.

Common Types of Cyberbullying

Cyberbullying can appear in many forms, but here are some of the most common:

- **Harassing messages**: Sending repeated, threatening, or unkind messages through texts, direct messages, or comments.
- **Spreading rumors or lies**: Posting fake information about someone to damage their reputation. This might involve saying the person did something bad or sharing a twisted version of a story.
- **Posting private information**: Sharing personal details or secrets without permission. This could be anything from someone's phone number to private photos or text conversations.
- **Impersonation**: Hacking into someone's account or creating a fake account pretending to be them. The bully might post harmful things to make the target look bad or cause them trouble with friends.
- **Exclusion**: Leaving a target out of online groups on purpose, such as group chats or gaming teams. While exclusion can happen in person too, doing it online can be more noticeable because it often shows exactly who was invited and who was not.

Why Cyberbullying Feels Overwhelming

Being bullied online can feel extremely stressful. First, because it can follow targets wherever they go—on their phone, tablet, or computer—they cannot find a safe spot just by leaving school or avoiding a certain place. They might wake up to new messages or posts that upset them. This ongoing nature of cyberbullying can make someone feel trapped or constantly on edge.

Second, the large audience of the online world can make the target feel deeply embarrassed. They might worry about classmates, relatives, or even strangers seeing cruel words or pictures. Each new share or like could mean another person is laughing at them. This fear of judgment can make them hesitant to talk about the problem or to ask for help, because they feel everyone has already formed an opinion.

Third, if the bully is anonymous, the target might suspect anyone of being behind the screen. This can lead to a sense of paranoia and distrust. They might think a friend or even a family member could be betraying them. This suspicion can harm friendships and make the target feel more isolated.

Potential Consequences for the Target
As with other types of bullying, cyberbullying can harm a target's emotional and physical well-being:

1. **Stress and anxiety**: Constantly checking their phone or social media in fear of new attacks can cause ongoing stress. This can lead to headaches, trouble sleeping, or a drop in ability to concentrate on daily tasks.
2. **Low self-esteem**: Negative messages might make a target doubt their worth. They could start believing the hurtful words they see, damaging how they view themselves.
3. **Depression**: If cyberbullying continues, it can contribute to feelings of hopelessness or sadness. The target might withdraw from friends or stop enjoying things that used to make them happy.
4. **Desire to avoid technology**: Some targets feel forced to leave social media or avoid their phone to escape harassment. While stepping away from online platforms can help in some cases, it can also isolate them from friends who use these tools to stay in touch.

What Drives People to Cyberbully?
The reasons someone might cyberbully can be similar to those for in-person bullying. They may seek power or control, or they might have anger they do not know how to handle. However, the online environment can intensify these motives:

- **Reduced sense of responsibility**: The screen creates distance between the bully and the target, making the bully less aware of the target's feelings. This can lead them to say things they would never say face-to-face.
- **Pressure to gain social approval**: In some peer groups, being bold or shocking online might bring attention and "likes" from bystanders. This can encourage more extreme behavior.
- **Revenge or frustration**: Some cyberbullies might feel they were wronged in some way and see online attacks as a form of payback. They might think, "They made me feel bad, so I'll do the same to them."

Impact on Bystanders in the Online World

Many people see cyberbullying happen through group chats, posts, or shared images. When bystanders see a cruel post but do not respond, they might feel guilty or uncertain. They may fear becoming the next target if they speak up against the bully. Others might join in by liking or forwarding hurtful content, feeling that this is just "online drama" or not a big deal. However, each share or comment can add to the damage done to the target.

Signs a Child Might Be Facing Cyberbullying

For parents, guardians, and teachers, it can be tricky to see cyberbullying because it often happens on personal devices. Still, some signs might point to a problem:

- **A sudden change in mood after going online**: The child might look upset or angry once they check messages or social media.
- **Avoidance of digital devices**: If they used to enjoy chatting with friends or playing online games but suddenly stop, it could mean they want to escape hurtful contact.
- **Withdrawing from social circles**: If the child stops hanging out with friends, it might be because they fear the bullying might spread offline.
- **Secretive behavior about their phone or computer**: While some privacy is normal, being overly guarded can suggest they are hiding embarrassing or hurtful exchanges.

What Parents and Guardians Can Do

Caring adults can take steps to help if a child is being bullied online:

- **Start open talks**: Ask if they have seen or experienced mean behavior online. Encourage honesty by staying calm and not overreacting. If a child worries that parents will take away their devices, they might hide the problem.
- **Know the apps and sites the child uses**: Understanding these platforms can help parents see how messages, posts, or chats work. This does not mean constantly spying on children but being aware of potential risks.
- **Help set privacy settings**: Show the child how to make their accounts private or block certain users. This can limit who can send them messages or see their posts.
- **Document evidence**: If bullying occurs, saving screenshots or messages can be important when talking to the school or, in serious cases, law enforcement.

- **Report and block**: Most social media platforms allow users to report abusive behavior. Encourage children to use these tools and to block the bully's account.

What Schools Can Do

Schools can also step up when cyberbullying spills into student interactions:

- **Teach online behavior**: Schools can explain to students that being respectful online is just as important as being respectful in person. Lessons about online safety, empathy, and standing up for others can make a big difference.
- **Encourage reporting**: Let students know how to report cyberbullying, whether it is happening to them or they see it happening to someone else. Teachers, counselors, or an online tip system can be used.
- **Respond quickly**: If a student shares that they are being bullied online, schools should take it seriously. Even though it occurs outside school grounds, it can affect the student's ability to learn and feel safe.
- **Offer support**: Counselors can check in with the target, provide emotional help, and guide them in handling the situation. Schools might also speak with the bully to figure out why they are acting out and how to stop it.

Teaching Digital Responsibility

Helping young people learn digital responsibility means showing them how to interact kindly online, how to respect others' privacy, and how to manage strong emotions without attacking someone else. A few ways to foster digital responsibility include:

- **Set screen time guidelines**: This is not a punishment but a step to encourage balance. Spending too many hours online can increase the chance of crossing paths with bullying behaviors or getting involved in heated exchanges.
- **Talk about consequences**: Children should know that screenshots can last forever. Cruel jokes or messages could be shared widely, harming their reputation as well as the target's feelings.
- **Encourage empathy**: Remind them that there is a real person behind each username or photo. Even if they cannot see someone's face, that person can still feel hurt.

- **Teach them to pause before posting**: Suggest that they take a moment to think about what they plan to write. Asking themselves, "Would I say this to someone's face?" can lower the chance of hitting "send" on something hurtful.

Handling Cyberbullying Incidents

When cyberbullying happens, there are steps that can help address the situation in a fair and safe way:

- **Gather details**: The target or a bystander can collect messages, comments, or screenshots that show what was said or posted. This creates a record of the bullying behavior.
- **Block the bully**: Many platforms have tools to block or mute accounts. This cuts off the bully's direct access to the target, though it does not always stop them from finding new ways to harass.
- **Report to the platform**: Social networks usually have guidelines against harassment. Reporting the bully's account can lead to warnings, account suspension, or removal of harmful content.
- **Tell a trusted adult**: If the target is a child or teen, sharing the situation with a parent, teacher, or counselor can help. Adults can offer guidance, support, and take steps to ensure safety.
- **Involve law enforcement if needed**: In severe cases—such as serious threats of harm, repeated harassment, or sharing private images—calling the police might be necessary.

Helping the Target Regain Confidence

Much like with other types of bullying, one of the key steps after cyberbullying is helping the target rebuild their self-worth. They might feel embarrassed that so many people saw the posts or messages. They could feel weak for not knowing how to handle it right away. Encouraging them to talk about their emotions and reminding them that they did not cause the bully's behavior can help. If needed, therapy or counseling can give them a safe space to discuss how the bullying affected their mood, friendships, or outlook on life.

Teaching Bystanders to Speak Up Online

The online world can be full of bystanders. Someone may see a rude comment left on a friend's post but feel unsure if they should do anything. Others might see a mean photo shared in a group chat and not want to seem like they are overreacting by saying it is not okay. Teaching young people that they can show kindness by speaking up is important. This does not mean they should put themselves in danger or respond with more insults. Instead, they can:

- **Show support to the target**: A quick private message saying, "I'm sorry this happened to you," can be comforting. It helps the target see they are not alone.
- **Report the post**: Even if they are not the target, bystanders can report harmful content to the platform moderators.
- **Avoid spreading hurtful material**: Do not share, forward, or like posts that attack or embarrass someone.
- **Preventing Cyberbullying Before It Starts**
  Preventing cyberbullying is easier than dealing with the damage it causes. Parents, schools, and community groups can:
- **Teach positive online conduct early**: Let children know that the internet is a shared space and that words can leave lasting marks.
- **Model good behavior**: If adults argue online or post rude comments themselves, children might follow that example. Seeing respectful online interactions from parents and teachers can set the right tone.
- **Encourage problem-solving skills**: Children who can solve conflicts calmly are less likely to turn to bullying. By learning to talk through disagreements or use compromise, they see the value in peaceful solutions.

Looking Ahead

As technology grows, so does the need to understand and address online harassment. New apps and platforms appear often, and bullies might adapt their methods. But we can stay informed and prepared by having open talks with children, setting clear rules, and taking action when bullying occurs. Cyberbullying may seem like just words on a screen, but it can be deeply painful for a target. By facing it directly, teaching kindness online, and promoting empathy, families and schools can help create a safer digital space for everyone.

The goal is not to scare young people away from technology, but to help them learn to use it wisely. When used well, the internet can connect us and give us access to knowledge we could never get otherwise. The key is to keep it a place where people can share, learn, and support each other, rather than tear each other down. By understanding how cyberbullying works and being ready to respond, we can protect ourselves and others from the harm it can cause.

Chapter 6: Psychological Effects on Targets

Bullying can damage a target's sense of self and peace of mind in ways that last far beyond the actual event. Children and teenagers who are bullied may face emotional wounds that shape how they see themselves and how they interact with others. These wounds might take the form of anxiety, sadness, or distrust, and they can continue long after the bullying itself ends. In this chapter, we will look closely at the psychological effects bullying can have on those who face it. We will also talk about steps that parents, schools, and friends can take to support those who have been hurt.

What Are Psychological Effects?
When we speak about psychological effects, we mean the impact on a person's thoughts, feelings, and behaviors. A single event of teasing might make someone feel upset for a short time. But repeated bullying can lead to deeper changes in a child's mind and emotions. Some people may experience frequent nightmares, constant worry about being teased again, or a strong fear of social situations. Others might start to doubt their own self-worth, feeling that they deserve this treatment or that there is something wrong with them.

Short-Term Effects
Some of the effects of bullying appear right away. For example, a child who is called names every day at school might develop stress. They could have a tight feeling in their chest or a churning stomach each morning before class. They may find it hard to pay attention because they are bracing for the next mean comment. In these cases, the bullying directly affects their learning and social growth. They might drop out of clubs or avoid the lunchroom to escape possible confrontations. This can lead to loneliness and isolation as they lose chances to connect with others.

Another short-term effect is feeling afraid in normally safe places. If a bully teases them in the locker room, the child might dread changing clothes for sports. If it happens on the bus, they might beg their parents for a ride to school. This fear can be overwhelming. As a result, some children might lie about feeling sick so they can stay home. Others might hurry through hallways with their head down, hoping not to be noticed. These actions show how targets change their behavior in an effort to avoid more hurt, even if it affects their daily routine.

Long-Term Effects
While short-term problems might ease after the bullying stops, there can also be deeper, long-term impacts. If a child has been repeatedly told they are stupid or worthless, they might carry that message into adulthood. They could find it hard to believe in their own talents or speak up in groups. Even as adults, they might feel anxious sharing opinions, fearing judgment or scorn. Research shows that people who were bullied as children can face higher risks of mental health challenges like depression or anxiety later in life. They might also struggle with forming healthy friendships or trusting their co-workers.

In some cases, the long-term effects can show up in unexpected ways, such as problems with anger control or trouble in relationships. If a person has learned to see the world as hostile, they might become defensive or withdrawn. They might assume that new people they meet will be unkind to them as well. This can affect their ability to maintain close bonds with friends, romantic partners, or co-workers. Though these effects do not appear in every target of bullying, they can be strong and lasting for many.

Self-Esteem and Self-Worth
One of the biggest areas impacted by bullying is self-esteem. Self-esteem is how a person values themselves. Bullying often breaks down a person's self-esteem by drilling in negative labels: "You're ugly," "You can't do anything right," or "Nobody likes you." Over time, targets might believe these remarks, feeling they have no strengths or good qualities. Low self-esteem can make them pull back from activities, thinking, "Why bother? I'm not good enough anyway." They might also become overly critical of themselves, blaming themselves for the bullying or for not stopping it.

This drop in self-esteem can set off a harmful cycle. The target might act shy or unsure in social situations, which can make them stand out even more to bullies who look for vulnerable peers. Each new act of bullying can further erode their confidence, trapping them in a loop of anxiety and self-doubt. Breaking this cycle often requires outside support from parents, teachers, or counselors who can help the target see their worth and remind them that bullying is not their fault.

Stress and Anxiety
Bullying can trigger strong stress responses in the target's mind and body. Stress is how the body reacts to threats or challenges, and bullying is certainly a threat.

A child might experience a racing heart or tense muscles when they spot the person who usually picks on them. This kind of ongoing stress can be exhausting. It can lead to trouble sleeping, as the child might worry about the next day's potential threats. Chronic stress can also weaken the immune system, causing them to get sick more often.

Anxiety is a type of intense worry or fear. Some targets might develop social anxiety, feeling very uneasy in any setting where they have to interact with classmates. Others might experience panic attacks, which can include sweating, shaking, and feeling like they cannot breathe. Anxiety can also make it hard to focus on schoolwork or enjoy hobbies. A child with ongoing anxiety might appear restless, irritable, or always on edge.

Feeling Sad or Hopeless
Depression can develop if bullying goes on for a long time without resolution. A depressed child might have trouble finding joy in daily life. They might seem tired or uninterested in things they once loved, such as sports, arts, or being with friends. They could have trouble eating or sleep too much or too little. In some cases, they might feel that their situation will never improve, leading to thoughts of wanting to escape life. These feelings can be very serious and require professional help.

It is important for parents, friends, and teachers to watch for signs that a child is feeling unusually sad or hopeless. Early support can make a huge difference. Small steps, like talking openly about what is happening or seeing a school counselor, might lighten the burden. Sometimes, professional therapy may help a child process painful emotions and learn coping strategies.

Trust Issues and Social Isolation
When someone is bullied, they might decide to keep to themselves to avoid being singled out again. They might push friends away, fearing they cannot trust anyone or that no one truly likes them. This isolation can lead to missing out on important parts of childhood, such as making memories with friends or joining teams or clubs. Over time, the lack of social connection can deepen their sense of loneliness.

Trust problems can also appear. If a friend stood by and did nothing during bullying, the target might believe nobody is dependable. They might wonder, "If my friend didn't help me, maybe others won't either." This feeling of betrayal can affect future friendships or relationships, as the target might expect abandonment or disloyalty. Sadly, this makes it harder for them to build meaningful bonds, because they stay closed off to new connections.

Effects on Schoolwork and Activities

A bullied child may lose interest in classes or activities that once brought them joy. Rather than enjoying a drama club or a sports team, they might avoid after-school programs to dodge bullies. Their grades could slip because they cannot concentrate or because they are skipping school more often. This can create added stress, as they might feel they are failing in school on top of dealing with harassment.

Activities like sports or clubs usually teach teamwork, friendship, and personal growth. If a child withdraws from them, they miss out on these positive experiences. This might limit their chance to build the self-confidence that can come from achieving goals or being part of a group that supports them. As a result, they may feel that they have nowhere to turn for encouragement.

Signs of Psychological Harm

Parents, teachers, and friends can watch for clues that a child is struggling with deeper emotional damage from bullying:

- **Sudden personality changes**: A once-outgoing child might become quiet and fearful.
- **Loss of interest**: They give up on activities they once found exciting.
- **Changes in mood**: Quick shifts from sadness to anger, or long periods of gloom.
- **Constant complaints of feeling sick**: Headaches, stomachaches, or other physical signs of stress.
- **Avoidance behaviors**: Hiding in the restroom at lunch, changing routes to class, or refusing to use social media.

Ways Adults Can Offer Support

Adults can do a lot to lessen the psychological damage bullying causes:

- **Keep lines of communication open**: Ask open-ended questions about their day and feelings. If the child seems hesitant, remain calm and patient.

- **Listen without judgment**: Show empathy by truly hearing what they say. Avoid phrases like, "You just need to be tougher." This can make them feel dismissed.
- **Seek professional help**: If the child shows signs of depression, severe anxiety, or other mental health struggles, consider speaking with a counselor, therapist, or doctor.
- **Work with the school**: If the bullying happens at school, talk to teachers or the principal. Ask what safety steps can be taken to protect the child while ensuring the bully is addressed.
- **Provide reassurance**: Remind the child that they are not to blame for the bullying. Emphasize their strengths and the things they do well.

Healthy Outlets for Emotions
Targets of bullying often hold a lot of anger, sadness, or fear inside. Finding healthy ways to release these feelings can help them cope:

- **Art or writing**: Drawing, painting, or writing can help them express the pain they are going through.
- **Music**: Playing an instrument or listening to calming songs might ease stress. Singing can also be a form of emotional release.
- **Sports and physical activity**: Exercise can reduce tension, release endorphins, and offer a sense of achievement when they hit a new goal or do well in a game.
- **Talking with a trusted friend or mentor**: Sometimes just voicing the problem can make it feel more manageable.

Peer Support
Friends can play a big role in helping someone heal from bullying. If a classmate notices their friend is upset, they can:

- **Offer an ear**: Listening can help the target feel less alone.
- **Encourage them to seek help**: Remind them that there are adults who care and can take steps to protect them.
- **Stand by them**: Walking together in hallways or sitting together at lunch can discourage bullies and make the target feel safer.
- Peer support groups or clubs at school can also be a place where students talk about bullying and learn ways to handle it. These groups might share advice or invite counselors to give talks. Knowing there is a safe place to open up can significantly reduce feelings of isolation.

Building Resilience

Resilience is the ability to bounce back from hardships. While bullying is never the target's fault, building resilience can help them handle challenges more easily. This does not mean ignoring the pain. Instead, it means recognizing strengths and learning strategies to cope with stress:

- **Self-talk**: Teach children to use words of encouragement about themselves. Instead of saying, "I can't do anything right," they can learn to say, "I'm working hard and I'll get better."
- **Setting small goals**: Achieving small goals, like completing a book or finishing a puzzle, can help build a sense of confidence that can counter bullying's negative messages.
- **Finding caring mentors**: A teacher, coach, or neighbor who shows genuine concern can give the target hope and a sense of belonging.

When Bullying Leads to More Serious Emotional Harm

Unfortunately, some targets face deep emotional pain that may include thoughts of hurting themselves or even ending their lives. This is a serious matter and must be taken very seriously. Warning signs can include statements about feeling worthless, withdrawing from all social contact, or giving away prized possessions. If someone mentions they wish they did not exist or that life is too hard, it is vital to seek professional help right away. Talking with a school counselor, calling a help line, or going to a mental health center can be life-saving steps.

Healing Takes Time

Recovering from bullying does not happen overnight. Even if the bullying stops, the target might still carry memories of unkind words or actions. They may replay the hurt in their mind, especially if the bullying lasted for a long period. Healing often involves many steps: talking about what happened, rebuilding lost confidence, and learning to trust others again. It may also include cutting off contact with the bully or finding new friends who bring positivity rather than meanness.

Helping Someone Who Was Bullied

If you know someone who faced bullying, there are ways to offer support:

- **Check in regularly**: A simple text or conversation can lift their spirits.
- **Invite them to activities**: Ask them to join a game, walk, or study session. Feeling included can help them regain trust and heal.

- **Encourage professional support**: If you see signs of severe sadness or hopelessness, talk to an adult or counselor.

A Community Approach

Addressing the psychological effects of bullying requires a community effort. Schools can create programs that teach empathy and kindness. They can also form groups where students help each other when they see or hear about bullying. Parents can share advice or resources with each other, so they are better prepared if their child is targeted. Local youth centers might hold talks or workshops to educate kids about the harm bullying can cause and the strategies they can use to respond.

Hope for the Future

Even though bullying can leave deep wounds, many children go on to heal and become strong individuals. They may use their experiences to help others, becoming mentors or leaders who speak against bullying in their communities. While the hurt they felt was real, it can also build compassion for those who are treated unfairly. By receiving the right support and learning coping skills, many targets discover that they are more than what the bully said or did to them.

This hope is important because it reminds us that bullying, while harmful, does not have to define a person's life. With caring friends, supportive adults, and a focus on building healthy coping strategies, targets can regain self-confidence. They can learn that their value is not decided by a bully's words or actions. They can also discover their strengths and direct their energy toward activities that bring them joy.

Looking Ahead

The psychological harm caused by bullying should never be underestimated. It can affect a child's emotions, thoughts, and behaviors for a long time. However, with awareness and action, these effects can be eased. Adults, peers, and communities can all help the child overcome fear, sadness, and shame. By offering understanding, access to counseling, and consistent care, we can support targets in finding a path toward a healthier future.

The key is early recognition and open dialogue. When children feel safe talking about their troubles, they are more likely to receive help in time. By learning the signs of distress, staying alert, and being willing to step in, we can greatly reduce the impact of bullying on mental health. The more we address the deeper reasons and effects of bullying, the better we can help those who suffer from it become resilient, confident, and able to thrive.

Chapter 7: Long-Term Consequences for Those Who Bully

Children and teenagers who bully might seem powerful in the moment, but their actions can bring serious costs as they grow up. While bullying often focuses on harm done to the targets, it is also important to look at how the bully can be harmed by their own behavior. Over time, people who continue to bully without being guided to change can develop patterns of aggression and other issues that follow them into adulthood. This chapter will explore the possible long-term consequences for those who bully, including trouble in school, social and emotional concerns, and difficulties in building a fulfilling life.

---

1. **Early Warning Signs**

Some children show early warning signs that they might bully others. These can include an attraction to rough behavior or using threats to get their way. While being physically or verbally aggressive does not always lead to long-term problems, it can be a signal that they need help developing healthier communication skills. If parents, teachers, or community members do not take these warning signs seriously, the child's habit of bullying can become fixed. Over time, this fixed behavior may guide how they deal with conflict and emotions, making aggression their first response when challenges arise.

2. **Academic Consequences**

Students who bully may not realize it, but their actions can interfere with their own learning. When they act out in class, they might be sent to the principal's office, suspended, or placed in separate learning programs. These punishments can interrupt their education, causing them to fall behind on schoolwork. In some cases, chronic misbehavior leads to expulsion, which can severely limit future academic opportunities. Children who bully might also get a reputation among teachers as "troublemakers," which can affect how teachers respond to them. While teachers are meant to treat all students fairly, a long record of bullying may cause some teachers to be extra strict or cautious, making the classroom experience tense and less supportive for the bully.

In the long run, these academic struggles can limit a bully's chance to attend higher-level schools or colleges. A weak academic record can keep them from certain scholarships or programs that would have offered better prospects. Sometimes, bullies also pay less attention in class because they are too focused on dominating or intimidating others. This focus on harming rather than learning can lead them to miss out on important skills that could help them in the future. As a result, they might leave school with fewer options for jobs or advanced education.

3. **Difficulty in Friendships and Relationships**

While it might look like bullies have friends—especially if they lead a group that follows them—they often struggle to build genuine, trusting friendships over time. A bully may act popular among peers who fear or admire them in school, but as people grow older, many do not want to stay close to someone who is aggressive or hurtful. Real friendship is built on mutual respect and concern, not intimidation. When classmates mature, they may see bullying as unacceptable and distance themselves from people who do it. Over time, the bully can find themselves with limited social support.

This pattern can continue into adult relationships. A person who learned that threats and force are the main ways to interact may try those methods in the workplace or in romantic partnerships. This can lead to serious consequences, such as repeated conflicts or even legal action if their aggression crosses the line. They may lose jobs or damage important personal bonds. Trust becomes hard to earn when a person has a history of hurting others. If the bully never learns to manage anger, share control, or handle problems calmly, they may struggle to keep long-term friendships or stable relationships.

4. **Emotional and Psychological Costs**

Sometimes, people think of bullies as fearless or uncaring. However, those who bully can face their own emotional and mental struggles. They might feel guilt, shame, or confusion about their behavior, even if they do not show it outwardly. If a bully's environment never addresses their aggression, they may not learn how to handle difficult emotions in a positive way. They can become stuck in a pattern of lashing out whenever they feel stressed, frustrated, or afraid.

In the teen years, these emotional struggles can include higher risks of alcohol or drug use, depression, and anxiety. A teen who bullies might try to escape feelings of guilt or anger by using substances. They might also experience internal conflicts if they realize that their aggressive habits lead to loneliness or rejection. Without help, these issues can deepen. Studies suggest that individuals with a history of bullying might face higher risks of certain mental health problems, though this does not happen to everyone. Still, the link between harmful behavior and emotional problems is strong enough that it cannot be ignored.

5. **Trouble with the Law**

Repeated bullying can escalate. As children grow older, bullying can become forms of criminal behavior if it involves physical harm, theft, or harassment that breaks local laws. A teenager who has learned to use threats or force to get their way might use the same tactics outside of school. If they join groups that encourage violence, they might become involved in fights or vandalism. These actions can lead to arrest, probation, or even time in detention centers. A criminal record can seriously affect future options for jobs, scholarships, and housing.

Even if the bullying never leads to serious crimes, small offenses can add up. Threatening messages online, destruction of property, or minor assaults can put someone on the police's radar. Employers often run background checks, and a reputation for aggression or lawbreaking can make it hard to find work. While not every child who bullies ends up on this path, the risk is higher if they do not receive proper support and guidance to change their behavior.

6. **Workplace Problems**

A bully who does not adjust their behavior may become an adult who shows aggression in the workplace. They might belittle coworkers, take credit for others' efforts, or use threats to maintain power. While some workplaces handle bullying strictly, others might ignore it, especially if the bully is in a position of authority. Over time, though, employees may file complaints, leave the job, or confront the bully. An adult who bullies coworkers can face lawsuits, demotions, or terminations. They can also end up on internal "watch lists," making it hard for them to move up or find new opportunities.

Furthermore, adult bullies might struggle with collaboration or communication. Many jobs require teamwork, compromise, and empathy. If a person's default approach is intimidation, they will find it difficult to lead teams or build strong working relationships. This can stall their career growth. They might go from job to job, never staying in one place long enough to succeed. Over time, this can result in financial instability and ongoing career frustration.

7. Family and Parenting Challenges

Individuals who bully often learn their behavior from the environment they grew up in, but they can also pass it on to their own children if they remain aggressive. A bully-turned-parent might use harsh discipline methods, yelling, or threats at home. This can create a cycle where their children, in turn, learn that force and fear are how you solve problems. These children may then repeat the same actions at school or in other settings, creating another generation that struggles with bullying.

This pattern can cause conflicts with partners or other family members who do not agree with harsh behavior. It can lead to separation, divorce, or strained family ties. If child protective services or other agencies become involved due to reports of aggression at home, the individual's personal life can face more problems. All of this makes it harder to build stable, loving relationships.

8. Lost Opportunities

When someone bullies, they may overlook chances to learn positive social skills, like empathy and patience. They might skip healthy outlets such as being part of a team, engaging in community service, or forming close bonds with mentors. These missed chances can reduce the bully's growth as a well-rounded individual. While others learn cooperation or kindness through group projects, the bully may just focus on controlling or dominating others. This single-track behavior can limit their personal development and keep them from discovering new interests or talents.

Lost opportunities also appear in education and the workplace. A bully might get suspended, losing valuable class time and missing out on critical lessons. If they gain a reputation for aggression, teachers or bosses might be unwilling to recommend them for special programs or promotions. Over time, the bully can feel stuck, blaming others for holding them back without recognizing that their own behavior is the problem.

9. **Isolation and Loneliness**

It might seem odd to say that a bully could feel lonely, but it happens. People might fear or avoid them. Friendships built on fear rarely last, and most folks do not want to keep being around someone who is unkind. After school, when cliques and social circles change, the bully may find that they have not developed genuine bonds. Classmates who once stayed close out of fear or peer pressure often move on.

In adulthood, this isolation can grow if the bullying behavior continues. Coworkers might avoid the person or refuse to socialize with them outside of work. Neighbors might keep their distance. Over time, the bully might notice that they have few people to rely on, which can lead to sadness or bitterness. Without addressing their behavior, they remain trapped in this pattern.

10. **Shame and Regret**

Not all who bully remain stuck in harsh behavior forever. Some recognize the harm they have done and feel regret. This can happen when they face real consequences or see how their actions have hurt people they care about. Regret can lead to shame, which can be overwhelming if they do not know how to repair the damage. They may want forgiveness but feel unable to ask for it. Sometimes, they might think it is too late to change.

This shame can hold them back from growing into a kinder person. Guilt can be paralyzing if they do not have the tools or support to make amends. In other cases, shame might be a turning point. They might decide to apologize to those they hurt and seek help from a counselor or a trusted mentor. With the right steps, it is possible to change harmful patterns and build better habits.

11. **Signs That a Bully May Need Help**
    - **Anger outbursts**: The child or teen becomes aggressive at small annoyances, hinting at deeper frustration.
    - **Lack of empathy**: They seem unable to see how their actions affect others' feelings.
    - **Obsession with power**: They often talk about being tough or in control.
    - **Frequent conflicts**: They get into arguments with teachers, classmates, or family members on a regular basis.
    - **Lying or blaming others**: They deny responsibility and place fault on everyone else, showing an unwillingness to learn from mistakes.

When these signs appear, caring adults can step in and offer guidance. Punishing the bully without teaching them new ways to handle emotions or solve problems may only make matters worse. Interventions that include counseling, skill-building activities, and family involvement can change the bully's path.

12. **Ways to Intervene and Promote Change**
    - **Counseling or Therapy**: Talking with a mental health professional can help a bully learn to deal with anger, fear, or insecurity in a healthier way. Counseling might also show them how their actions hurt others, helping them develop empathy.
    - **Behavior Plans**: Schools can create plans that outline clear rules and consequences. They can also set goals for positive interactions. When the bully meets these goals—like resolving a conflict peacefully—they might earn small privileges or positive feedback.
    - **Anger Management Training**: Classes or one-on-one sessions can teach a bully to recognize the signs of anger before it explodes. They might learn to step away from a tense situation, take slow breaths, or use words to talk through disagreements.
    - **Mentorship Programs**: A coach, teacher, or community member can become a steady role model, showing the bully how to treat others with respect. This personal connection can encourage the bully to see themselves in a more positive way.
    - **Parental Involvement**: If parents use harsh or aggressive methods at home, they may also need guidance. Helping the entire family learn calm communication skills can lower aggression overall. This approach might stop the bully from receiving mixed messages—such as being punished for bullying at school but seeing it at home.
13. **Positive Outcomes for Those Who Change**

Even though bullying can have serious long-term effects, people can learn to behave differently. When they gain insight into why they acted aggressively, they might find better ways to handle conflict. Learning to see other people's viewpoints can help them form real friendships. As they experience the benefits of kindness, they might realize that force is not the only way to feel strong. Some former bullies become helpers to others who struggle with anger. They can share their experiences and explain why they decided to abandon harmful behavior.

Real change often requires consistent effort, empathy-building lessons, and supportive adults who do not give up on the person. In some communities, peer-led programs teach kids to talk openly about the harm bullying causes. Former bullies might step up to say, "I used to act this way, and I know now it was wrong." Hearing this honesty from a peer can be powerful for students who are still stuck in bullying patterns.

14. Avoiding Blame and Shaming

While those who bully should be held responsible, endless blame or shaming often does not fix the root problem. Telling them they are "bad" might only make them feel resentful or hopeless. Instead, adults can separate the harmful actions from the whole person. They might say: "What you did caused hurt. Let's talk about why it happened and how to make it right." This approach focuses on the behavior rather than labeling the individual forever. It also opens a path for growth and improvement.

15. Building New Habits

To avoid serious long-term consequences, the bully needs to replace old habits with new ones:

- **Learning to apologize**: Taking responsibility for harmful words or actions teaches respect.
- **Practicing conflict resolution**: Role-playing peaceful ways to solve problems can build confidence in using calm language instead of threats.
- **Finding healthy outlets**: Sports, art, or community service can offer a sense of achievement without hurting anyone.
- **Reflecting on triggers**: If a bully knows certain things upset them (like feeling left out), they can plan how to handle those feelings before they lead to aggression.

16. Role of Schools and Communities

Schools and communities that have clear anti-bullying rules help reduce the odds of long-term harm to both targets and bullies. When bullies face real consequences for harmful actions—such as suspension, mandatory counseling, or losing privileges—they learn that aggressive behavior is not acceptable. However, these consequences should come with a plan to teach them better coping methods. Community centers, sports teams, and youth groups can also create positive peer cultures where bullying is not welcome. By offering bullies structured ways to connect with others and learn respect, communities help them avoid a future filled with conflict.

17. Hope for the Future

It might seem that a child or teen who bullies is doomed to a life of aggression and regret, but that does not have to be the case. Yes, bullying can lead to lost friendships, academic trouble, legal issues, and emotional struggles. But with the right guidance, many people can turn their behavior around. Recognizing that bullying stems from deeper needs—like wanting control or dealing with anger—helps adults address the real causes. When bullies build healthier skills, they may find themselves better able to handle stress and form honest connections.

18. A Shared Responsibility

The best outcomes often happen when parents, schools, and community members share the duty of guiding the bully toward positive change. Parents can look for parenting classes or therapy if they see signs of unresolved anger in the home. Teachers can offer extra support, noticing when a child is making small improvements. Community leaders can organize programs that promote empathy and kindness. All these efforts send a clear message: we care about you, but we will not allow you to harm others.

19. Conclusion: Learning a Healthier Way

Those who bully others face many potential long-term consequences: poor academic performance, social isolation, mental health struggles, trouble with the law, and more. However, these outcomes are not inevitable. Many bullies can learn to change if they have a chance to understand their behavior and receive guidance on controlling anger, building empathy, and forming positive relationships. Adults and peers can play a major role by setting firm boundaries, providing consistent consequences, and offering pathways to healthier actions.

By recognizing that a bully's behavior can ruin their own future as well as harm others, we gain motivation to intervene early. Helping them develop respect and kindness is not just about protecting targets—it is also about giving the bully a shot at a better life. This balanced approach shows that no one has to remain stuck in harmful patterns. The hope is that, with awareness, support, and strong values, those who used to bully can grow into individuals who treat others with fairness and understanding.

Chapter 8: School Environments and Bullying

Schools are central places for learning and growth. They shape the minds of students through lessons, activities, and social relationships. Because children and teenagers spend so many hours at school, the overall school environment influences whether bullying thrives or fades. A healthy school environment fosters respect, offers clear rules, and provides students with chances to develop strong social skills. On the other hand, a poor school environment might allow bullying to go unnoticed or unpunished. In this chapter, we will look at how the culture, policies, and everyday routines of a school can affect bullying, and what steps can be taken to make sure students are safe and supported.

What Is a School Environment?

The term "school environment" covers everything from the buildings themselves to the attitudes of teachers, staff, and students. It includes rules, discipline procedures, and the emotional tone within classrooms and hallways. A positive school environment might be described as one where students feel welcome and able to speak freely without fear of being picked on. In such schools, teachers and staff treat students fairly, and students know what is expected of them in terms of behavior.

Signs of a Positive School Environment

- **Clear rules against bullying**: Posters, assemblies, and discussions about respect make it clear that bullying is not accepted.
- **Adult involvement**: Teachers, coaches, and counselors actively watch for harmful behavior. They step in quickly when a student reports a problem.
- **Open communication**: Students feel comfortable talking to adults about their worries. They know they will be taken seriously and not blamed.
- **Inclusive activities**: Clubs, teams, and school events encourage all students to join in, regardless of background or skill level.
- **Visible care**: Staff offer kindness and support, greet students by name, and notice signs of stress or sadness. Students see that adults care about them, which reduces the fear of speaking up.

Signs of a Negative School Environment

- **Vague or inconsistent rules**: No clear message on what bullying is or how it will be handled.
- **Limited adult supervision**: Hallways, cafeterias, or playgrounds might have few adults watching student interactions. Bullying can happen unnoticed in these areas.
- **Fear of reporting**: Students worry they will be punished or that nothing will change if they speak up, so they stay silent.
- **Favoritism or unfair treatment**: Teachers or staff might ignore certain students' complaints or take sides without hearing everyone involved.
- **Hostile atmosphere**: Students feel tension, noticing that classmates often insult each other or that teachers scold students harshly.

In a negative environment, bullying can become part of daily life. Students may see it as normal to tease or exclude classmates. Without teachers stepping in, bullies learn they can get away with causing harm.

Policies That Make a Difference

Having a clear anti-bullying policy is important. This policy should define what counts as bullying, including physical, verbal, and online forms. It must outline the steps staff will take when bullying is reported, such as:

- **Investigating**: Talking to the target, the bully, and any witnesses.
- **Documenting**: Keeping written records of each incident and any actions taken.
- **Notifying parents**: Alerting the families of both the target and the bully.
- **Applying consistent consequences**: If bullying is confirmed, consequences should match the severity of the action. This could include loss of privileges, counseling, or suspension for serious cases.

When these policies are carried out fairly, students see that their school stands against bullying. They understand that bullying is not a personal problem the target must handle alone but a violation of school rules that concerns everyone.

Role of School Leaders

Principals and other leaders can set the tone for the entire school. If a principal takes bullying seriously and trains staff on how to address it, teachers feel more prepared to intervene. Conversely, if leaders overlook complaints or claim bullying is just part of growing up, the staff may follow this mindset. Effective school leaders make a point of:

- **Allocating resources**: Hiring enough playground or hallway supervisors, for example, or providing training to teachers on handling conflict.
- **Creating reporting channels**: Having an easy way for students to send in anonymous tips about bullying can help catch problems early.
- **Reviewing data**: Checking how many bullying reports come in each month, where problems occur most, and what the outcomes have been.
- **Adjusting strategies**: If bullying remains high in a certain hallway or during a certain time of day, leaders can add extra staff or cameras to watch that area.

Teacher Training and Response

Teachers are often on the front lines of bullying. However, they do not automatically know the best methods to handle it unless they receive guidance. Training can cover:

- **Spotting less obvious types of bullying**: Emotional bullying or exclusion can be harder to notice than physical fights. Teachers should learn to look for signs like a student always sitting alone or a group whispering and giggling when another student talks.
- **Calm intervention**: When teachers see bullying, they should step in without anger or panic. They might separate the students, hear each side briefly, and then move the discussion to a private space.
- **Following school policy**: Teachers need to know the steps to document bullying incidents, inform leaders, and apply any needed consequences or next steps.
- **Encouraging empathy**: Through classroom projects, teachers can help students practice thinking about how their actions affect others. This can involve group activities or role-playing respectful behavior.

Student-Led Actions

Students themselves can be important in shaping a positive school environment. Peer-led clubs or groups can promote kindness and look out for classmates who seem isolated. Such groups might organize awareness events or create simple pledge boards where students promise to treat each other with respect. These activities send a strong message that bullying is not "cool" or admired.

In some schools, older students mentor younger ones, teaching them to handle conflicts with words instead of fists. Younger students might feel safer knowing they can approach an older mentor who understands how they feel. This bond across grade levels also helps create a sense of unity in the school.

Involving Parents and Families

Families are a key part of the school environment, even if they are not there physically. Schools can reach out to parents by:

- **Sending newsletters or emails**: These can explain the school's approach to bullying and suggest ways parents can support it at home.
- **Hosting workshops**: Inviting parents to talk about bullying, share ideas, and learn strategies to talk with their children.
- **Encouraging communication**: Reminding parents that if they suspect their child is bullying or being bullied, they should inform the school. Early notification can help resolve problems before they get worse.

When parents know the school has a firm anti-bullying stance, they feel safer letting staff know of any concerns. This helps close the gap between home and school, ensuring that both are on the same page.

Physical Layout and Supervision

Sometimes, the structure of a school building can impact bullying. Crowded hallways, hidden corners, or unsupervised bathrooms can be places where bullies strike. Schools can address these risks by:

- **Posting monitors in busy areas**: Staff members can keep an eye on popular gathering spots.
- **Installing cameras**: While cameras do not replace adult presence, they can discourage bullying in hallways or other common spaces. They also help confirm reports if an incident occurs.
- **Adjusting schedules**: If bullying often happens during a certain transition (like after lunch), administrators might stagger release times so fewer students are in the hall at once.

- **Improving playground design**: Ensuring supervisors have clear sightlines and removing hidden spots where children can be isolated.

Climate Surveys and Student Feedback

One effective tool for improving the school environment is conducting climate surveys. Students, staff, and sometimes parents can fill out questionnaires about how safe they feel, how often they see bullying, and whether they think adults respond effectively. By reviewing the results, school leaders can find specific areas that need attention. For instance, if many students say they do not trust teachers to handle bullying, training or new procedures might be put into place.

Regular surveys, done annually or semiannually, can track progress over time. If the numbers show that students are feeling safer, it suggests that changes are working. If bullying reports remain high, leaders can delve deeper to figure out why.

Building Empathy in the Classroom

Some of the most meaningful efforts to prevent bullying happen during class time, when teachers can include empathy-building activities. For example, a teacher might:

- **Share stories**: Reading books or showing short videos that depict individuals in tough situations can spark discussions about feelings.
- **Use role-playing**: Students can act out scenarios involving conflict, then practice resolving them with kind words.
- **Hold open discussions**: Inviting students to talk about moments when they felt left out or upset helps them see that everyone has feelings.
- **Praise caring acts**: When a student helps a classmate, the teacher can draw attention to it, showing the class that kindness is noticed and appreciated.

Peer Conflict vs. Bullying

Schools also need to teach students (and staff) the difference between normal peer conflict and bullying. Conflicts happen when classmates argue or disagree, but neither side holds a clear power advantage or uses repeated threats. Bullying, on the other hand, often involves one person who has more influence or control targeting someone weaker. Schools can use lessons and examples to clarify these differences. Doing so prevents bullies from dismissing repeated aggression as "just conflict" while also helping students learn how to handle normal disagreements in respectful ways.

Early Intervention

One reason a strong school environment helps is that teachers can catch small acts of meanness before they grow into severe bullying. A child might start by lightly mocking a classmate, and if the teacher calmly intervenes, the child may learn that such behavior is not tolerated. If the teacher fails to step in, the child might assume it is acceptable and escalate the behavior. By intervening at the start, schools can prevent a cycle of intimidation from forming.

School Events That Promote Respect

In addition to day-to-day efforts, schools might hold events to reinforce a culture of kindness. These could include:

- **Assemblies with guest speakers**: People who share personal stories about bullying can help students see its real effects.
- **Team-building days**: Activities where classes mix up groups, giving students a chance to know peers they might rarely speak with.
- **Art or writing contests**: Students can create projects about respect, which can be displayed around the school.
- **Group service projects**: Working together to help the community can bond students and teach cooperation.

Such events stand out in students' memories and remind them that the school values respectful treatment of everyone.

Responding to Reports

When a student reports bullying, the school's reaction is crucial. If staff handle it quickly and fairly, the target feels validated and the bully sees that there are consequences. If the school dismisses the complaint, students get the message that speaking up does not help. A well-run process might look like this:

- **Listening carefully**: An adult hears the details of the situation without interrupting or accusing the target of lying.

- **Asking clarifying questions**: Who was involved? Where and when did it happen? Were there any witnesses?
- **Thanking the student**: Reporting takes bravery, so a simple "Thank you for telling me" can encourage future honesty.
- **Separating those involved**: If needed, the bully and target are kept apart until the issue is sorted out.
- **Gathering more information**: The adult talks to witnesses, reviews security footage, or checks social media (if it happened online).
- **Deciding on action**: Depending on the severity, consequences could include a warning, contacting parents, or other steps as outlined in the school's policy.
- **Following up**: Checking in with the target afterward to ensure the bullying has stopped.

Protecting Targets from Backlash

One worry is that once a target reports bullying, the bully might retaliate. Schools can protect the target by keeping details as private as possible and monitoring any interaction between them and the bully. Seating charts or schedules might be adjusted so they have minimal contact. The school can also encourage supportive peers to walk with the target in hallways. This close watch may need to continue until staff are sure the bully has changed their behavior.

Keeping a Record

Documenting each reported case of bullying helps the school see patterns. If certain students appear as bullies multiple times, staff can plan stronger interventions. Records can also show if a certain spot, like the lunch line or bathroom, is a hotspot for bullying. Being organized with data allows school leaders to target their efforts effectively.

Teaming Up with Community Resources

Sometimes, bullying issues may be too big for a school to handle alone. If a student who bullies shows signs of anger or deeper emotional problems, outside counseling might be suggested. If a family faces tough circumstances—such as homelessness or violence at home—the school might link them to community organizations that offer food, shelter, or family support. By viewing the child as part of a larger situation, schools can better address the roots of the bullying.

Building Respectful Habits for the Future

A school environment can either encourage aggressive habits or teach peaceful ones. When students see kindness modeled by teachers and staff, they are more likely to practice it themselves. Over the years, daily routines like greeting each other, working in diverse groups, and recognizing good deeds shape students into people who are caring and alert to injustice. This influence extends beyond the school's walls, because children carry these lessons into their neighborhoods and future workplaces.

A Shared Commitment

Creating a school environment that stands against bullying is not a quick fix. It takes time, resources, and a shared commitment from teachers, students, parents, and administrators. But the outcomes are worth it: reduced fears, healthier friendships, improved academic performance, and a sense of safety that allows every child to learn. Schools are not just buildings; they are social ecosystems where children spend a large part of their early years. By investing in a kind atmosphere, schools can help students grow into adults who do not accept aggression as normal.

Moving Forward

A positive school environment is one of the strongest defenses against bullying. When rules are clear, teachers are ready to act, and students support each other, harmful behavior struggles to survive. Instead of focusing only on punishing bullies after the fact, schools can take a broad approach—teaching empathy, understanding peer conflicts, involving families, and promoting open communication. These steps ensure that as children grow, they develop the skills and attitudes needed to treat others with kindness and respect.

Creating these changes may seem challenging, but even small adjustments—like a teacher praising kind words, or a principal holding regular check-ins with students—can make a difference over time. The goal is a school environment where everyone feels welcome, and where no one has to fear being teased, excluded, or threatened. By building a culture of respect each day, schools can protect students from bullying and guide them toward healthier ways of interacting that will serve them for the rest of their lives.

Chapter 9: Family Dynamics and Prevention

Families play a central role in shaping how children see themselves and how they interact with others. A warm, stable home can guide children toward caring behaviors and respect for others. On the other hand, a tense or aggressive household may teach children that bullying or anger is a normal way to solve problems. In this chapter, we will look at how family relationships, parenting styles, and daily habits can help prevent bullying from taking root. We will also discuss ways parents and siblings can create supportive settings where each person learns healthy skills for handling conflicts and feelings.

---

1. **Why Family Dynamics Matter**

Family is often the first group where a child learns how to behave. They watch how parents and siblings communicate, solve disagreements, and express feelings. If they see people handling stress by yelling or throwing items, they might believe those actions are acceptable elsewhere. If they see calm, respectful talks during disputes, they begin to learn that approach themselves.

A home atmosphere sets patterns. When children see parents show kindness, they understand that caring about others is important. If they see siblings gently resolve a misunderstanding, they learn that mistakes can be fixed without name-calling. Conversely, if they notice one sibling often getting their way through bullying at home, they might copy that behavior at school. These family interactions serve as a first example of how to treat others.

2. **Parenting Styles and Their Influence**

Researchers often look at parenting in categories, such as:

- **Authoritative**: Warm but firm. Parents who use this style set clear rules and follow them, but they also listen to the child's viewpoint. Children in these households often learn that rules matter, yet they also feel valued.
- **Authoritarian**: Very strict, with little warmth. Children may follow the rules out of fear, but they might not learn empathy or understanding. Sometimes, they become angry or harsh because that is what they see from adults.

- **Permissive**: Very warm, but with few rules or limits. These parents might let children do as they please with little guidance. While children might feel loved, they can have problems controlling their impulses. This may open the door for bullying behaviors, as children might not learn boundaries.
- **Uninvolved**: Parents who are distant, showing neither warmth nor structure. Children in these homes can feel alone or unnoticed. They might turn to bullying to get attention or as a response to unresolved frustration.

No household is purely one style at all times, and real life is more complex. But understanding these broad types can help us see why some families produce children who bully. If a child does not learn to respect others' feelings at home, or if they are under constant threat of punishment with no empathy, they might struggle with healthy relationships later.

3. **How Family Stress Can Affect Behavior**

Many families face stress—whether it is from financial problems, health issues, or major changes like moving. During stressful times, parents might feel exhausted and have less patience with their children. This can lead to harsh words or yelling more than usual. If a child regularly hears a parent shouting when problems arise, they may imitate that approach when they feel upset. Over time, this can develop into bullying behaviors if the child sees that shouting or threatening leads to results.

Families can reduce this risk by finding ways to handle stress. This might include seeking support from relatives, neighbors, or community resources. It might also mean setting aside a few minutes each day to talk as a family about any worries. When children see that parents are trying to handle stress without blaming or hurting others, they are more likely to copy that model. Even if the family situation is tough, a calm or caring moment can go a long way in showing a better path.

4. **Sibling Relationships and Bullying**

Bullying can happen among siblings. An older sibling might use size or age to push a younger sibling around. Sometimes, teasing among siblings can be playful, but it can also become harmful if one sibling is constantly the target of insulting words or aggressive acts. If a child learns to bully a sibling without consequences, they may try the same tactics outside the home.

Parents should watch for signs of sibling bullying. A child might avoid spending time with their sibling, cry frequently after interactions, or complain about feeling unsafe at home. If parents notice these signs, they should step in. Clear rules at home—such as "No name-calling" or "No hitting"—can help set boundaries. Parents can also encourage siblings to solve problems through polite conversation or by taking turns calmly explaining their viewpoints. When parents teach fair ways to settle disagreements, siblings learn that aggression is not the proper way to deal with conflict.

5. **Encouraging Empathy at Home**

One of the strongest tools against bullying is empathy—being able to understand and care about how someone else feels. Families can build empathy in many ways:

- **Show kindness in daily life**: Children pick up on small actions, like a parent helping a neighbor or comforting a friend.
- **Talk about emotions**: Parents can label their own feelings in a calm manner: "I'm feeling frustrated right now because I can't find my keys." This shows children that it is normal to identify and share emotions rather than lash out.
- **Ask about the child's day**: Simple, open questions like "How did that make you feel?" or "How do you think your friend felt?" prompt a child to think about feelings.
- **Use stories or movies**: While watching a show or reading a story together, ask the child how the characters might feel and why. This practice helps a child step into someone else's shoes.

When empathy becomes a normal part of family talk, children are less likely to turn to bullying. They begin to see peers as people with real feelings, not just targets to push around.

6. **Setting Family Rules to Prevent Bullying**

Clear family rules can help prevent bullying both inside and outside the home. These rules do not need to be long or complicated. Examples might include:

- **"Use respectful words."** This means no name-calling, mocking, or insults toward anyone in the family.
- **"Keep hands and feet to yourself."** This stresses that physical aggression is not acceptable.

- **"Help each other solve problems without yelling."** When a conflict arises, encourage family members to slow down, listen to each other, and propose fair solutions.
- **"Apologize when you are wrong."** This can reduce tension and teach children that mistakes happen, but ownership is important.

Such rules should apply to everyone—parents too. When parents model these rules, children see that the family takes kindness seriously.

7. **Encouraging Good Communication**

Communication is key to preventing bullying. If children feel comfortable talking with parents about their problems, they are more likely to mention if they feel pressured to bully or if they are being targeted by others. Families can promote open communication by:

- **Holding regular check-ins**: Maybe at dinnertime or before bed, ask each child how they are feeling and if anything is worrying them.
- **Listening closely**: When a child is sharing something, focus on them. Put aside phones or other distractions. Show genuine interest.
- **Avoiding judgment**: If a child confesses they made a mistake, try to stay calm. Talk about the consequences and how to fix it rather than shouting or labeling them "bad."
- **Offering solutions together**: If a child is upset about a classmate, brainstorm together how they might handle it next time. Let the child come up with ideas while you guide them toward respectful choices.

This open-door approach builds trust. Children are more likely to admit wrongdoing or ask for help when they believe parents will listen and support them.

8. **Preventing Bullying Through Self-Control Skills**

Sometimes children bully because they have trouble managing their impulses. They might hit or yell before they fully think about the impact. Parents can help children develop self-control in everyday life:

- **Teach "pause and breathe"**: When a child is upset, encourage them to take a deep breath before responding. This short break can help them calm down and avoid saying or doing something they regret.

- **Offer choices**: Giving a child limited choices ("Would you like to do your homework now or in 15 minutes?") teaches them to think through decisions, which can help them handle bigger conflicts more calmly.
- **Promote patience**: Activities that build patience—such as puzzles or board games where they must wait their turn—can gently train children to handle frustration without aggression.
- **Model calm behavior**: Children watch how adults handle anger. If a parent yells at traffic or storms around when annoyed, a child learns that outburst pattern. If a parent stays calm, the child sees that it is possible to pause and think.

Handling Past Bullying Incidents at Home

If a parent discovers their child has been bullying others, it is crucial to address it early. Ignoring the issue might cause it to get worse. Steps to handle it include:

- **Staying calm and firm**: Explain what you heard about the bullying and why it is not allowed.
- **Asking the child's side**: Hear how they describe the situation, but do not excuse hurtful actions.
- **Discussing impact**: Help them see how the target might feel. Use questions like, "How do you think the other person felt when that happened?"
- **Problem-solving**: Brainstorm better ways they can handle conflicts or boredom next time. Maybe they were teasing out of frustration or to seem cool. Guide them to more respectful ways to fit in or express anger.
- **Enforcing fair consequences**: This might mean apologizing to the target, losing privileges for a time, or performing a helpful task to make up for their actions.
- **Seeking help if needed**: If the bullying is severe or ongoing, a counselor might provide extra support for the child to manage anger or stress.

When Your Child Is a Target of Bullying

Family can also be a refuge for a child who is being bullied elsewhere. Parents can take a few key steps:

- **Show understanding**: Believe the child's account. Thank them for telling you. Being brushed off can deepen a target's sense of isolation.

- **Gather details**: Ask what happened, where it happened, who was there, and how often it has happened.
- **Work with the school**: If the bullying occurs at school, contact the teacher or counselor. Provide specific details. Ask about any safety measures the school can provide.
- **Help the child cope**: Encourage them to spend time with supportive friends, join clubs or activities they enjoy, and practice standing tall or speaking confidently.
- **Build resilience at home**: Remind them that they have worth. Find things they do well—whether it is sports, art, or solving puzzles—and praise their efforts. Feeling capable in one area of life can reduce the emotional sting of bullying.

Balancing Love and Boundaries

Some parents worry that being strict about bullying might harm their relationship with the child. In reality, children often feel safer when parents set clear limits. It shows that the parents care enough to teach right from wrong. Balancing love and boundaries means:

- **Being affectionate and supportive**: Give hugs, listen to ideas, share fun times together.
- **Holding them accountable**: If they hurt someone, they must take responsibility. Explain that making amends is part of learning.
- **Avoiding excessive punishment**: While discipline is necessary, going too far with anger or long punishments can cause more rebellion or shame. Aim for consequences that fit the behavior and teach a lesson.
- **Emphasizing hope**: Tell the child you believe in their ability to act kindly. This keeps them from feeling permanently labeled as "the bad kid."

Teaching Conflict Resolution

Households that promote positive conflict resolution give children real tools to avoid bullying. Parents can do simple exercises, such as:

- **Role-playing**: Pretend you and the child disagree on something. Model how to speak calmly, listen, and find a fair compromise.
- **"I feel" statements**: Teach children to say, "I feel upset when you call me that name. Please stop." This is more constructive than trading insults.

- **Shared problem-solving**: If two siblings both want the same toy, guide them to come up with a solution. They might decide to set a timer and take turns.
- **Praising good solutions**: When a child handles a disagreement without yelling, notice it: "I like how you talked with your brother instead of arguing."

By practicing these skills at home, children are less likely to use aggression or threats at school or in friendships. They grow more confident in their ability to speak up and resolve clashes peacefully.

Addressing Technology at Home

With the rise of online platforms, many bullying incidents happen digitally. Families should talk openly about safe ways to use phones and computers. Some tips:

- **Set boundaries**: Decide how many hours per day children can be online. Keep tech devices in shared areas, if possible, to discourage harmful chats or posts.
- **Discuss respectful online speech**: Remind children that teasing or threatening online can hurt just as much as in person.
- **Check privacy settings**: Teach them to make profiles private and to avoid sharing personal information.
- **Encourage open conversations**: If a child sees or experiences hurtful behavior online, they should feel free to show a parent without fear of losing device privileges unless truly necessary.
- **Be aware of apps and games**: Know which social media sites and online games the child uses. Some games may have chat features that can enable bullying. Keep an eye on potential red flags.

When parents are involved, children learn that family values apply online too. They see the internet as an extension of real life, requiring the same respect and care.

When Outside Help Is Needed

Sometimes, even well-intentioned families struggle if a child consistently bullies or is bullied. These problems might be tied to deeper issues like trauma, mental health concerns, or ongoing stress. In such cases, seeking outside help can make a big difference:

- **Therapy or counseling**: A counselor can help a child learn to express anger or anxiety in healthier ways. They might also build the child's self-esteem if they feel stuck in a negative role.
- **Support groups**: Some communities have groups where parents and children can share experiences about bullying and learn strategies together.
- **Educational workshops**: Schools or local groups may offer parenting classes that focus on empathy, communication, and discipline methods.
- **Help from mentors**: Trusted relatives, family friends, or community leaders can be extra guides, especially if the child lacks a supportive adult at home.

Cultural and Family Differences

Families differ in their backgrounds, traditions, and beliefs. Some cultures might handle discipline with strict rules, while others prefer a softer approach. The key is finding a way that teaches respect without encouraging fear or aggression. Parents who come from places where harsh discipline is the norm can still adapt to new ideas, such as using reason and empathy. By mixing the best elements of their own heritage with practical tips for positive parenting, families can shape an environment where bullying does not flourish.

Building a Support Network

To maintain a peaceful home atmosphere, parents benefit from having their own support network. Stressful events can make it harder to remain patient or consistent. By having other adults to talk to—friends, grandparents, or members of a community group—parents can release tension in a safe way instead of letting it explode around children. This network can share advice on how to handle tantrums, discipline, or sibling fights. They might also watch the children at times, giving parents a break to recharge.

Teaching Respect Through Chores and Teamwork

Daily chores and family tasks can be a chance to teach responsibility and cooperation. Children who learn to contribute may grow in empathy and respect. For instance:

- **Team cleaning**: Have siblings or parents and children tidy up a room together, discussing who does which part. This teaches compromise and shared effort.
- **Cooking together**: Planning and making a family meal is a good way to practice patience and working together.
- **Caring for younger siblings**: Older children might help read a book to a younger sibling. This can teach kindness and patience.

These routines give children a sense of belonging and remind them that the household runs on shared effort, not on one person bossing the others around.

Modeling Apologies and Forgiveness

Mistakes happen in every family. Parents might lose their cool, or siblings might argue. One important step is showing how to repair the bond afterward. Parents can model apologies by saying, "I'm sorry I raised my voice. That wasn't right. I was upset, but I should have taken a moment to calm down." This simple statement teaches children that apologies are not a sign of weakness, but a step toward better understanding. It also encourages children to accept apologies and forgive, rather than holding grudges. This cycle of apology and forgiveness can keep conflicts from turning into repeated bullying.

Looking Forward

Family life is not perfect, and children can still face bullying risks even in supportive homes. But when families create an atmosphere of kindness, communication, and fair limits, children are better prepared to handle peer pressure or disagreements. They know how to talk about problems, how to say "I'm sorry," and how to see the feelings of others. This foundation helps prevent bullying behaviors and builds resilience if the child ever becomes a target of bullying.

No single method works for every family, but the themes of empathy, clear boundaries, and open talks are useful everywhere. By focusing on these areas, parents and siblings can become a strong front against bullying. They show children that respect starts at home and continues in the outside world. With these habits in place, the family becomes a place of safety and growth, lowering the chances of harm for everyone involved.

Chapter 10: Community Involvement and Intervention

Bullying does not exist only within families or schools. It happens in neighborhoods, parks, sports fields, and community centers as well. A child who feels unsafe in the community might avoid leaving home or exploring new activities. Meanwhile, a child who bullies might act out in local programs without facing much accountability if the wider community does not respond. In this chapter, we will look at how communities can spot, reduce, and address bullying. We will also talk about the roles of local leaders, businesses, youth organizations, and regular neighbors in building safer spaces for everyone.

---

1. **Why Communities Matter**

Children grow and interact not just in their homes or schools but in the larger area around them. They attend parks, libraries, local events, and clubs. Each place can either support kindness or allow bullying to go unchecked. By working together, community members can set norms for positive behavior. When children see that adults in all parts of their lives stand against bullying, they learn that harming others is not accepted anywhere.

Communities often have resources—like youth centers, sports leagues, or public libraries—that bring together children from various schools and neighborhoods. This mixing can be a chance for new friendships to form. However, it can also create places where bullies find fresh targets or use aggression to show off. Community involvement can guide children toward healthy social skills and show them new ways to handle disagreements.

2. **Identifying Bullying Outside of School**

Parents and neighbors may notice bullying in places like:

- **Playgrounds**: Some children might dominate the play area by pushing others off swings or mocking them in front of peers.
- **Youth sports**: A strong player might belittle less skilled teammates, or team members might gang up on an unpopular player.

- **Community centers**: In free hangout areas, older kids might pick on younger ones with taunts or physical threats.
- **Online forums within communities**: Local chat groups or gaming servers can also be zones where cyberbullying occurs.

When adults see these incidents, they can either step in or turn away. Stepping in calmly can prevent further harm and show that caring behavior applies everywhere, not just in school.

3. **Local Leaders and Law Enforcement**

In some cases, ongoing bullying can break the law, such as when it involves threats, severe harassment, or physical assault. Law enforcement officers can play a role if the problem goes beyond typical childhood conflicts. However, involving law enforcement is not always the first step. Many communities prefer to handle mild bullying with guidance and mediation unless it escalates. Still, having a good connection between schools, community centers, and police can be helpful. This connection might include:

- **Youth officers**: Some places have officers who focus on youth outreach, visiting schools or attending neighborhood events. They can talk about safety, respect, and ways to report severe bullying.
- **Community policing**: Officers might walk around playgrounds or chat with residents to build trust. If a child or teen sees an officer as friendly, they may be more likely to ask for help if they feel unsafe.
- **Referral systems**: Police might link families to counseling or local programs if they see a pattern of aggression in a child.

The idea is not to treat every bullying case like a crime. Rather, it is about offering support and making sure serious threats do not slip through the cracks.

4. **Role of Youth Organizations**

Local youth groups, like scouting clubs, faith-based programs, sports teams, or art clubs, can strongly influence whether bullying is reduced. Leaders of these groups can:

- **Set a respectful tone**: At the start of each season or program, leaders can lay out clear expectations—no insults, no shoving, and no hateful words.

- **Supervise carefully**: Coaches and group leaders can watch for signs of bullying, such as a child always picking on the same teammate or spreading rumors about someone.
- **Encourage teamwork**: Many youth organizations succeed when members cooperate. By praising kids who help each other or show respect, leaders guide the group to see that meanness is not valued.
- **Handle incidents promptly**: If bullying happens, a coach or leader should address it right away. They might speak privately to those involved, remind them of the rules, and, if needed, involve parents.
- **Host skill-building workshops**: Some groups invite experts to speak about managing anger, improving communication, or practicing empathy. This can help kids learn positive habits they will use in all parts of life.

By creating a caring atmosphere, youth programs can become places where children learn life skills and feel safe from bullying. They can also teach children from different schools or backgrounds to get along and appreciate each other's differences.

5. **Community Centers and Safe Spaces**

Community centers often provide spaces where children can gather after school, on weekends, or during summer breaks. These centers can reduce the risk of bullying by offering:

- **Structured activities**: Boredom sometimes leads to bullying. Giving children games, crafts, or sports to focus on can keep them engaged in positive ways.
- **Adult guidance**: Trained staff members or volunteers who observe interactions can step in if they see teasing or pushing. They can also guide kids to talk through disputes.
- **Peer support**: Kids who attend the same center regularly can build friendships and look out for one another. A supportive peer group can discourage bullying if they stand up against it.
- **Counseling or mentoring**: Some centers might offer free or low-cost counseling services for families who need extra help with conflict or stress.

When community centers set clear policies about respect, bullying is less likely to thrive. A child who might act tough outside can face immediate pushback from staff and other children who do not accept that behavior.

6. **Local Businesses and Public Areas**

Bullying is not limited to official programs. It can happen in shops, fast-food places, or any spot where kids gather. Businesses can help prevent bullying by:

- **Training staff**: A store manager can teach employees how to respond if they see a child harassing another child in their store.
- **Posting guidelines**: Signs saying "We welcome all. Please treat each other with kindness" can set an inclusive tone.
- **Creating family-friendly environments**: Well-lit spaces, cameras, and polite staff can reduce the chance of bullying going unnoticed.
- **Partnering with community groups**: Local shops might sponsor anti-bullying events or help spread information about local programs that teach respect.

These steps show that kindness is valued throughout the community, not just in certain places. Children notice when adults consistently uphold respectful norms, and they might adjust their behavior accordingly.

7. **Neighborly Vigilance**

Sometimes, the simplest help comes from people who live in the area. If a neighbor sees repeated bullying on the street, they can approach the children in a calm manner to ask if everything is okay. They can also inform parents if they know them. Neighbors who turn a blind eye to bullying let it continue, but those who take small actions can make a significant difference. For instance, a neighbor could:

- **Invite kids to play in a supervised yard**: If the neighbor is comfortable, they might offer a safe area for basketball or other activities, keeping an eye out for harmful behavior.
- **Stay observant**: If they see a child being harassed daily at the same time, they might report it to parents or community leaders.
- **Offer a listening ear**: Sometimes, an older neighbor might chat with kids and give gentle guidance about fairness and respect.

These actions build a sense of shared responsibility. Children learn that the entire community, not just teachers and parents, cares about their well-being.

8. **Community-Wide Campaigns**

Many places organize campaigns to spread awareness about bullying. These can include:

- **Posters and signs**: Local shops, libraries, and youth centers can display messages like "Stop Bullying—Speak Up."
- **Workshops or fairs**: The community might hold an event with booths, where families can learn about dealing with bullying, conflict resolution, and mental health resources.
- **Public speakers**: Sometimes, people who have overcome bullying or have expertise in child behavior give talks. Hearing real stories can help both kids and adults understand the impact of bullying more deeply.
- **Social media efforts**: Local authorities or groups might share tips on staying safe, reporting bullying, and supporting targets.

By joining in these campaigns, children see that many people stand against bullying. They may also find resources they did not know existed.

9. **Faith Communities**

Churches, mosques, synagogues, and other faith communities can be strong allies in preventing bullying. Many faith traditions teach kindness, respect, and concern for others. Leaders and members can:

- **Host discussions**: Youth groups within these communities can talk about bullying and how it relates to the group's teachings on compassion.
- **Offer counseling or mentorship**: Faith leaders are sometimes approached by families in distress. They can counsel parents and children or refer them to professional help.
- **Organize service projects**: Activities that involve helping neighbors in need can build empathy and teamwork among children. By working together, they see the power of kindness in action.

10. **Empowering Bystanders**

A key part of reducing bullying is teaching bystanders that they have power to respond. Communities can run workshops or produce materials that explain safe ways to step in when someone is bullied. For children, this might include:

- **Telling an adult**: Encouraging them to find a staff member, coach, or neighbor right away.
- **Not joining in**: Making clear that laughing or posting mean videos online supports the bully.
- **Offering comfort**: Reaching out to the target afterward with a kind word or an invitation to hang out. This lessens the target's sense of isolation.

Bystanders often worry about becoming targets themselves. Communities can highlight that if enough bystanders speak out, the bully's power shrinks. Even quietly reporting the behavior can be a big help.

11. Support for Children Who Bully

Children who bully outside of school settings need help too. If the community simply bans them from programs without addressing root causes, they may seek other places to continue the same actions. Instead, organizations can:

- **Sit down with the child**: Find out what is causing the aggression. Are they dealing with anger at home, peer pressure, or past hurt?
- **Assign a mentor**: A caring adult, such as a coach or volunteer, can spend extra time with the child, teaching them positive social skills.
- **Set clear boundaries**: Let the child know that continued bullying will lead to consequences, but also offer steps to make things right, like apologizing or doing a helpful task.
- **Communicate with parents**: Make sure the family knows the child's actions and has resources to address them.

This approach treats the child as someone who can change with guidance, rather than labeling them forever.

12. Handling Severe Incidents

Sometimes, bullying goes beyond teasing to serious harassment or violence. In these cases, community members may need to take stronger action:

- **Involving law enforcement**: If there is a direct threat, severe injury, or repeated harassment, the police might need to step in.
- **Obtaining restraining orders**: If a bully threatens someone's safety, the family might get a legal order to keep the bully away.
- **Seeking professional intervention**: The bully may need therapy or anger management sessions. The target might need counseling to cope with fear or trauma.
- **Alerting community leaders**: If a spot becomes known for repeated bullying, local leaders can improve security or supervision.

Though these steps can feel extreme, they protect everyone's safety and send a clear message that serious harm is not tolerated.

13. **Developing Anti-Bullying Skills for Adults**

Adults often want to help but do not always know how. Communities can offer short training sessions on de-escalating conflicts, reading children's body language, or responding to bullying calmly. This training might be for:

- **Coaches and referees**: They can learn what to do if players start insulting or pushing each other on the field.
- **Library or recreation staff**: They might see arguments among teens who gather after school. Knowing how to intervene right away can stop bullying in its tracks.
- **Bus drivers**: If kids ride a local bus for school or after-school programs, the driver might witness teasing or fights.
- **Local business owners**: They can spot signs of bullying in or around their shops. If they know a clear process—like contacting parents or local community officers—they can respond in a safe, consistent way.

14. **Helping Targets in the Community**

Children who are bullied outside school may feel they have nowhere to turn if they do not want to get parents or the school involved. Community members can create safe options, such as:

- **Youth hotlines or text lines**: Where children can call or text about bullying they face at a park or in a local group. Volunteers can provide guidance and connect them with help.

- **Anonymous reporting**: A local website or phone line to report bullying incidents so leaders can address them, possibly by adding more supervision or talking to those involved.
- **Social gatherings**: Well-organized block parties or holiday events can bring neighbors together and build friendships. Children who know each other and see parents cooperating may be less likely to bully or feel alone.

Feeling backed up by the community can give targets more courage to speak out. They realize they are not alone and that adults are willing to protect them.

15. Bringing People Together Across Ages

Community programs that unite different age groups can reduce bullying as well. When children spend time around older teens or adults who show kindness, they absorb these norms. For instance:

- **Reading buddies**: Younger kids pair with older youth or adults for reading practice at the library. They see that older people can be caring mentors, not threats.
- **Community gardening**: Group activities that involve planting or cleaning up a park teach cooperation. (Avoiding the restricted words: do not use synonyms for "cultivate.")
- **Multi-age sports**: Non-competitive leagues where older players help younger ones learn the basics. This fosters a sense of mentorship and responsibility rather than intimidation.

When kids from various backgrounds cooperate, they learn to respect differences. This helps weaken the "us vs. them" mindset that can fuel bullying.

16. Local Media and Awareness

Local news outlets, blogs, or social media pages can help spread stories of successful anti-bullying efforts. By highlighting positive outcomes—like a youth sports team that turned around its teasing problem—media can show other community members that change is possible. They might also interview experts on child development or share tips with families who suspect their child is bullying or being bullied.

17. Funding and Resources

Sometimes, communities want to expand anti-bullying programs but lack funds. In such cases, they can:

- **Apply for grants**: Government or charitable groups might offer money for youth outreach, safe community projects, or mentorship programs.
- **Partner with local businesses**: A shop might sponsor sports uniforms or help fund a workshop on conflict resolution.
- **Hold fundraisers**: Neighborhood events like bake sales or fun runs can bring people together to raise money for anti-bullying efforts.
- **Work with local charities**: Nonprofit groups focused on children's welfare might supply training materials or volunteers to run after-school programs.

With financial help, communities can expand their ability to watch for bullying, train staff, and support families.

18. Building a Culture of Respect

Ultimately, the goal is to shape a culture where bullying is not seen as "kids being kids," but as a harmful act that hurts everyone. This involves repeated messages of respect from many sources: posters, sports coaches, local leaders, business owners, neighbors, and parents. It is about more than just telling kids "Don't bully." It is about showing them that caring about others is the normal and expected way to behave.

This cultural shift takes time. A few people may resist changes or think that minor teasing is harmless. But with consistent education and stories of real harm caused by bullying, more community members begin to see the importance of stepping in early.

19. Success Stories

Communities around the world have created safe, inclusive spaces by focusing on respect:

- A small town that organized a monthly "Friendship Day" at the local community center, drawing children from different neighborhoods to do

team activities. Over time, the sense of unity grew, and bullying incidents dropped.
- A sports league that set strict rules against name-calling and had coaches talk to players every week about sportsmanship. Bullies faced consequences like sitting out the next game, but they also got a chance to learn better ways to channel competition.
- A group of concerned parents who took turns supervising the local playground in the summer, making sure everyone felt safe. They also planned casual picnics, so families got to know each other. Once neighbors formed friendships, they were more likely to watch out for each other's children.

These examples show that small actions can add up. When communities unite, children see that bullying is not tolerated, and they are given new ways to behave.

20. **Moving Forward**

Preventing bullying is not just a task for families or schools. The entire community must come together. Community centers, local leaders, coaches, and neighbors all have a role to play in making public areas safe and welcoming. By watching for signs of aggression, setting clear expectations, and supporting both targets and those who bully, communities can reduce harmful behavior. This shared effort creates a place where children can grow, learn, and build friendships without fear.

When children feel safe in their neighborhood, they have more freedom to explore positive activities. They might join a sports team, learn new skills at a community center, or just spend time outside with friends. These experiences help them develop confidence and social skills, lessening the likelihood of bullying. At the same time, bullies can find role models and guidance to shift their behavior. In the end, a caring community benefits everyone, teaching respect and understanding that will last well beyond childhood.

Chapter 11: The Role of Empathy

Empathy is the ability to understand or feel what someone else is going through. It means seeing the world from another person's point of view and caring about their feelings and experiences. When empathy is strong, people are less likely to tease or harm each other because they realize that their words and actions can cause real pain. In this chapter, we will look at how empathy helps prevent bullying, ways to grow empathy in both children and adults, and how it can lead to more caring and peaceful relationships.

What Is Empathy?
Empathy involves more than just feeling sorry for someone. It is about genuinely trying to see the situation through their eyes. For example, if a classmate is sad because no one picked them for a game, empathy helps you imagine how lonely and embarrassed they might feel. This understanding can push you to include them or offer kind words. Without empathy, people may overlook others' pain or see it as unimportant. That lack of concern can leave room for harmful actions, like bullying.

Why Empathy Reduces Bullying
When people understand the hurt that bullying causes, they are less likely to engage in it. A bully might tease someone to seem cool or strong, but if they truly understood the sadness or fear their target feels, they might pause. Empathy can act as a barrier against meanness. It reminds potential bullies that the target has feelings just like them—nobody likes being made fun of or pushed around. Empathy also motivates bystanders to step up. If they see someone being hurt, empathy drives them to help or report the behavior to an adult.

How Empathy Helps the Target
When a target of bullying feels that others empathize with them, it can lighten their emotional burden. They realize they are not alone. A simple "I'm sorry that happened" or "Are you okay?" can give them strength to seek more help. Targets who sense that their feelings matter are more likely to speak up. They may tell a teacher, parent, or friend that they need support. This sense of connection can stop further harm, because bullies often rely on their targets feeling powerless.

How Empathy Helps Those Who Bully
A child who bullies may struggle with anger or other problems they do not know how to handle. If they learn empathy, it can change their perspective. They begin to see that harming others causes real damage. This understanding can open the door to healthier ways of handling stress. For instance, instead of teasing someone to release anger, they might decide to talk to a counselor, pick up a safe hobby, or confide in a trusted adult. Empathy can guide them to ask, "How would I feel if someone did this to me?"

Empathy and Bystanders
Bystanders are those who witness bullying. Empathy helps bystanders realize the target's pain and step forward rather than staying silent. If a bystander sees someone crying after being insulted, empathy can drive them to comfort that person or get help from a teacher. Sometimes, bystanders are afraid the bully will target them next. But when they truly grasp the hurt caused by bullying, they might feel that staying silent is not right. This can result in a group of caring onlookers who protect the target and discourage the bully.

Teaching Empathy to Children
Empathy does not always appear on its own. Children often learn it by watching and practicing. Here are some ways adults can teach empathy:

- **Label Emotions**: When a child is upset, help them name what they are feeling, such as "angry," "sad," or "worried." Recognizing emotions in themselves can help them recognize similar feelings in others.
- **Read Stories Together**: Books or short stories with characters facing problems can spark conversations about how each character feels. Ask children questions like, "Why do you think this character is upset?"
- **Role-Play**: Let children act out different scenarios. For example, pretend one person is left out of a game. Then pause and ask, "How do you feel?" or "What do you think would help?"
- **Highlight Kind Acts**: If a child shares a toy with a sibling, point it out: "That was very thoughtful. How do you think they felt when you let them play?" This shows that caring actions matter.

Empathy in Schools
Schools can make empathy part of their lessons. Teachers might:

- **Use Group Activities**: Working in teams can help students notice each other's ideas and feelings.
- **Encourage Class Meetings**: A short discussion each week about fairness or helping others can remind students that everyone's feelings count.
- **Have Students Share Their Stories**: Let children talk about times they felt hurt. Hearing personal accounts can open eyes to how words or actions affect someone's heart.
- **Praise Thoughtful Behavior**: When a student stands up for a classmate, teachers can thank them. This sends a message that empathy is valued as much as academic success.

Empathy in Families
Families have a big influence on empathy. Parents and siblings can show empathy in daily life by:

- **Listening Actively**: When someone in the family is upset, give them full attention. Let them talk without rushing to judge or fix everything right away.
- **Validating Feelings**: Even if you do not agree with why they are upset, you can still say, "I understand you feel this way." This helps them know you care.
- **Exploring Solutions Together**: If a problem arises, discuss possible solutions calmly. Ask, "How do you think each person would feel if we do that?"
- **Being Fair and Firm**: Setting rules against unkind words or hitting teaches respect. Then, if someone slips, explain the harm it causes instead of just punishing them. This approach blends empathy with guidance.

Empathy in the Community
Communities can foster empathy by organizing events that encourage understanding:

- **Public Talks**: Speakers who share experiences with bullying can help neighbors understand the deep hurt it causes.
- **Workshops**: Sessions on communication skills, feelings, or stress management can show both children and adults ways to show empathy in everyday life.

- **Service Projects**: Helping the elderly, cleaning up public spaces, or collecting supplies for those in need can help children see the value of caring for others, even if they are strangers.

Challenges to Growing Empathy

Not everyone learns empathy quickly. Some people might have grown up in harsh environments or faced trauma that makes them wary of others' feelings. They might block out empathy because it feels risky to care. Children who have gone through a lot of stress may seem cold or unfeeling. They might also misunderstand others' emotions due to limited social practice. In such cases, small steps help. A caring mentor or counselor can guide them by gently exploring emotions and providing patient support.

The Role of Forgiveness

Empathy connects to forgiveness, because understanding someone's struggles can make it easier to let go of anger. This does not mean ignoring harm. Rather, empathy can help both the target and the bully see that problems can be solved without ongoing hatred. For instance, if a bully apologizes sincerely and shows they regret their behavior, the target might find it easier to move forward. On the other side, if the target can empathize with a bully's hidden pain (like issues at home), they might see the bully in a new light. This does not excuse the bullying but can reduce ongoing conflict.

Using Empathy to Solve Conflicts

Conflicts do not always mean bullying. Sometimes, two people just disagree. Empathy can transform a heated argument into a calm talk. By pausing to ask, "How does this look to you?" they each get a glimpse of the other's perspective. When each side feels heard, they are more open to finding a middle ground. In this way, empathy can be a tool for preventing small arguments from turning into bigger issues. Schools, families, and youth groups can teach a simple process:

10. Let each person speak without interruption.
11. Ask them to restate the other's point of view in their own words.
12. Encourage them to say how they feel.
13. Brainstorm solutions that respect both people's feelings.

This method helps children become comfortable with empathy as a normal part of solving problems.

Empathy and Emotional Health
Learning empathy can improve a child's emotional health. When children practice noticing and naming feelings in others, they become better at handling their own feelings too. Empathy can lower stress levels, because children who feel understood are less lonely or anxious. They also have an easier time making friends, since they show care and kindness. Over time, these positive interactions help them grow self-confidence and reduce the urge to lash out.

Activities to Strengthen Empathy
Below are some simple activities families or educators can use:

- **Feelings Chart**: Hang a chart with different faces that show emotions like happy, sad, scared, or angry. Have children point to or name which face matches their current mood. Then let them guess the mood of a character in a story or a person on TV.
- **Kindness Boards**: Put up a small board where kids can write or draw kind things they saw someone do. This helps everyone notice empathy in action.
- **Shared Goals**: Plan a project (like a group puzzle or a small craft) where each person's help is needed. While working, encourage children to check on how everyone else is feeling.
- **Perspective-Taking Games**: Show a picture of a situation—a kid dropped their ice cream or someone lost a toy—and ask, "How do you think they feel? What do they need right now?"

Empathy in the Digital World
Many interactions happen online, and empathy is just as important there. Text messages, social media posts, and gaming chats can hurt someone if we forget that real people read them. Children can learn online empathy by:

- **Thinking Before Posting**: Ask, "Would I say this to the person's face?"
- **Recognizing Tone**: Words in a chat can be misunderstood if the reader cannot see your facial expression. Teaching kids to be mindful of phrasing helps avoid accidental hurt.
- **Standing Up Online**: If they see someone being mocked in a comment section, they can either post a polite reply to show support for the target or report the post if it breaks rules.

- **Resisting Gossip**: Forwarding or sharing embarrassing pictures can spread harm. Teaching children not to pass on mean content is part of digital empathy.

Empathy for Yourself

It is also important to have empathy for your own feelings, sometimes called self-compassion. If someone is too harsh with themselves—always calling themselves stupid or worthless—they may lack patience for others, too. By treating oneself with care and understanding, it becomes easier to extend that kindness outward. A child who can say, "I am upset, but I can learn from this mistake," is less likely to take out their frustration on someone else.

Empathy Through Listening

One of the easiest ways to show empathy is to listen well. This means:

- **Facing the person**: Look at them, not your phone or other distractions.
- **Letting them finish**: Do not cut them off. Give them time to express themselves.
- **Asking questions**: If you are not sure about something, ask politely for more details. This shows genuine interest.
- **Checking understanding**: Repeat what they said in your own words to see if you got it right. You can say, "So you feel hurt because they left you out, is that correct?"

Good listening helps build trust. People feel respected when they are heard, which reduces tension and improves relationships.

Genuine Concern vs. Pretending

Empathy must be sincere. If someone pretends to care but does not truly mean it, the target might sense the dishonesty. For empathy to have a real effect, the concern should be honest and caring. That does not mean you must agree with everything another person does. You can dislike their actions but still recognize their feelings. A sincere approach is more likely to bring understanding and resolve tensions.

Long-Term Benefits of Empathy

As children with empathy grow into adults, they often show:

- **Better Communication**: They know how to talk things through instead of resorting to threats or name-calling.

- **Stronger Friendships**: Friends trust and rely on them because they are caring and fair.
- **Improved Leadership**: Leaders who care about group members' feelings tend to solve conflicts peacefully and inspire respect.
- **Deeper Community Ties**: Empathetic people often volunteer, help neighbors, and stay involved in local causes.

In all these ways, empathy fights against bullying and spreads goodness. It nurtures harmony wherever people gather, making repeated harm less likely.

Moving Toward an Empathetic Culture
Building empathy is an ongoing process for individuals, families, schools, and entire communities. It may start with small actions, like praising a child for comforting a friend or encouraging group members to consider each other's feelings in a dispute. Over time, these habits can grow into a culture where empathy is normal and bullying feels out of place. This culture shift can reduce conflict, build deeper bonds, and give everyone a chance to feel safe and understood.

When empathy is woven into daily life, children find that they do not need to put others down to feel strong. They learn that helping someone feel better can bring its own sense of fulfillment. Bystanders, too, become more confident in standing up for what is right. In this kind of environment, bullying has fewer places to hide. People are watching out for one another, ready to step in with genuine concern. Even when mistakes happen or tempers flare, empathy can lead everyone back to calmer, kinder ground.

Chapter 12: Building Self-Worth and Resilience

Feeling good about ourselves (self-worth) and being able to bounce back from hard times (resilience) are important for everyone. These qualities help people face struggles in healthier ways and reduce the likelihood of falling into harmful behaviors like bullying. Children and teenagers who believe in their abilities and feel confident about who they are often deal with problems without hurting others. If they do face teasing or conflicts, they have tools to stand up for themselves or seek help. This chapter will explain what self-worth and resilience are, why they matter, and how families, schools, and communities can help children build them.

Defining Self-Worth and Resilience

- **Self-Worth**: This is how much value people place on themselves. Children with healthy self-worth feel they matter. They respect their own abilities but are also honest about where they need to improve. They do not see mistakes as proof they are useless. Instead, they see them as normal parts of learning.
- **Resilience**: This means handling setbacks or stress without giving up. Resilient children can manage disappointment or conflict, then return to a calmer state of mind. They still feel sadness or frustration, but they cope with these feelings in a healthier way. Over time, resilience lets them grow stronger and wiser from challenges rather than being crushed by them.

Why These Qualities Lower Bullying

- **For Targets**: A child with strong self-worth may be less likely to believe hurtful words. They might think, "That insult doesn't define me." Such children are also more likely to speak up or tell an adult rather than feeling powerless.
- **For Those Who Bully**: A child who feels content and valued has less need to bring others down. Bullying can be a way to feel powerful if you do not believe in your own strengths. Resilience helps them handle anger or envy without attacking someone else.

- **For Bystanders**: If bystanders feel confident in themselves, they might be braver about standing against bullying. A strong sense of self can push them to do what is right instead of worrying about losing popularity.

Building Self-Worth at Home
Parents often have the first chance to help children see their value. Some tips include:

- **Praise Effort, Not Just Results**: Instead of saying, "You're so smart," say, "You worked really hard on that puzzle." This teaches children that improvement comes from trying, not from being naturally perfect.
- **Encourage Independence**: Let children make age-appropriate choices, like picking clothes to wear or deciding a weekend activity. This shows trust in their judgment.
- **Focus on Strengths**: Help children see what they are good at, such as drawing, sports, or being a good friend. Reminding them of their successes can build confidence.
- **Permit Safe Mistakes**: If a child tries something and fails, do not rush to fix it. Let them learn from the error. This helps them see that a setback does not define who they are.

Fostering Resilience at Home
Resilience grows through consistent support and practice:

- **Model Calm Reactions**: If parents handle stress by staying calm, children learn to do the same. For example, if a parent breaks a dish, they might say, "I'm upset, but let's clean it up and move on."
- **Teach Problem-Solving**: When challenges come up—a missing school item or a conflict with a sibling—guide the child to brainstorm solutions. This process helps them see that problems can be solved step by step.
- **Build a Routine**: Having consistent meal times, bedtimes, and study times gives children stability. This foundation makes it easier for them to handle surprises or stress.
- **Encourage Flexibility**: Sometimes plans change. Let children experience small changes or disappointments and learn to adapt. They might realize that being flexible can lead to new fun ideas or solutions.

Self-Worth and Resilience in Schools
Schools can boost these traits in many ways:

- **Safe Classroom Environment**: When teachers treat students kindly and set fair rules, children feel secure enough to take risks in learning. This can strengthen their self-worth.
- **Team Projects**: Group tasks encourage children to rely on each other and discover personal strengths. If they face hurdles, they learn resilience by trying again together.
- **Supportive Feedback**: Teachers who give constructive notes, like "Try adding more examples here," help students feel they can improve rather than that they failed.
- **Leadership Opportunities**: When students can lead a class discussion, organize a small event, or tutor younger children, they see that their skills are valuable to others.

Handling Disappointments in School

Disappointments are normal. Maybe a child does not make the team or earns a lower score than hoped. This is a chance to build resilience. A teacher or counselor might say:

- **"Let's talk about what went well."** Focusing first on positives helps them see they did some things right.
- **"What can we learn from this?"** Reflecting on the experience without shame can lead to better strategies next time.
- **"I believe in your ability to improve."** Encouraging words let the child see the setback is not the end of their growth.

Activities That Build Self-Worth

Families and schools can introduce tasks that help children notice their abilities:

- **Personal Hobby Time**: Whether it is painting, coding, gardening, or playing an instrument, hobbies let children discover strengths outside of classwork.
- **Sharing Achievements**: A child could keep a small "success journal" where they jot down daily wins—big or small. Over time, this list reminds them of their growth.
- **Helping Others**: Doing simple acts of service, like reading to younger kids or cleaning up a shared space, shows children they have something to give to others. This lifts their sense of worth.

Strengthening Resilience Through Challenges
Some parents try to shield children from all difficulty, but facing manageable challenges helps them develop resilience. Here are a few ideas:

- **Structured Risk-Taking**: Let them try a new sport or a difficult puzzle. If they fail, guide them to try again or learn from mistakes.
- **Chores and Tasks**: Assign tasks that match their age, like washing dishes or taking care of a pet. Dealing with the ups and downs of tasks helps them become more responsible.
- **Outdoor Adventures**: Simple outdoor play can teach them to adapt to different weather or solve minor problems—like finding a new path when the main trail is muddy.

Avoiding Overprotection
Too much protection can weaken resilience. If a parent always fights the child's battles or does their homework for them, the child misses a chance to grow stronger. Of course, it is good to guide and assist when truly needed, but stepping in for every small bump keeps children from learning to cope. They may enter adolescence feeling helpless, and that can lead to either becoming a bully (in an attempt to feel in control) or becoming easily victimized because they lack problem-solving skills.

Self-Worth and Bullying Prevention
When children feel good about themselves, they are less likely to let cruel words define them. A child with strong self-worth might respond to an insult by calmly walking away or by telling an adult. They do not see the insult as proof that they are unlovable. Also, a child who feels worthy does not usually crave the quick rush of power that bullying gives. Their confidence comes from their own achievements or healthy relationships, not from humiliating others.

Resilience and Recovering from Bullying
If a child is bullied, resilience helps them heal. They understand that the bully's actions do not measure their true worth. They might reach out to a teacher or parent for help rather than suffering alone. Even if they feel sad or scared, their resilient mindset can guide them to think, "This is hard, but with help, I can get through it." Recovery might involve talking to a counselor, leaning on friends, or learning self-defense if physical bullying is a risk. Resilience supports them in not giving up on friendships, clubs, or school because of fear.

Role of Friends and Peers

Friends can either boost or break self-worth and resilience. Supportive friends:

- **Cheer each other on**: They say kind words when a friend is upset.
- **Push each other to improve**: They challenge each other in a friendly way to try new things.
- **Offer a safe place to share feelings**: They listen without mocking or spreading secrets.

Unsupportive peers might tease a friend for failing, laugh at their fears, or ignore them when they are upset. Teaching children to pick friends wisely can protect their sense of self.

Community Programs That Help

After-school programs, sports teams, or music lessons can provide extra places for children to find strengths and practice resilience. Caring coaches or mentors often notice a child's talent and say, "You have a knack for this," which can be a huge self-worth boost. They can also model how to handle losing a game or messing up a performance without giving up. Such environments teach that success is about ongoing effort, not instant results.

Handling Negative Self-Talk

Sometimes, children say harsh things to themselves like, "I'll never be good at this," or "I'm stupid." Parents and teachers can help by:

- **Gently Correcting**: "You're not stupid. You just need more practice with this skill."
- **Offering Evidence**: "Remember last week when you solved that tough math problem?"
- **Teaching Balanced Thoughts**: "It's okay to say, 'I'm still learning how to do this.' That means you believe you can grow."
- **Focusing on Progress**: Remind them of small steps they have taken and how far they have come.

Resilience in Everyday Life

Resilience does not only show up in big events. It appears in daily actions. For example:

- **Waking Up on Time**: On mornings when it is hard to leave bed, resilience helps a child push through tiredness.

- **Trying a New Hobby**: They might fail at first, but they keep at it until they get better.
- **Sharing with Siblings**: Even if siblings argue, resilience helps them move past disagreements and remain close.
- **Adapting to Changes**: If a family moves to a new home, a resilient child might feel sad but is open to exploring the new neighborhood.

Encouraging a Growth Mindset

A growth mindset is the idea that abilities and intelligence can improve through practice. Children with this mindset see challenges as steps to becoming better. If they fail a test, they do not label themselves as dumb; instead, they consider what they can do differently next time. This mindset supports both self-worth ("I'm capable of learning") and resilience ("I can bounce back from setbacks"). Parents and teachers can reinforce a growth mindset by praising persistence more than natural talent.

Involving Children in Decisions

When children have a say in decisions that affect them, they develop a sense of control, which boosts self-worth and resilience. This might mean:

- **Family Discussions**: Let them share their opinions on weekend plans or daily routines. Even small choices help them feel responsible.
- **Classroom Rules**: Involving students in making or reviewing class rules can make them feel that their voices matter.
- **Group Activities**: When kids plan events, they practice handling tasks and dealing with obstacles that come up.

What If Self-Worth Is Low?

Some children have very low self-esteem due to bullying, family stress, or other issues. Signs might include avoiding social contact, constant self-criticism, or giving up easily. In these cases, extra steps are needed:

- **Professional Support**: A counselor or therapist can help them see their good qualities and find healthier ways to handle hurt.
- **Small Goals**: Encourage them to do one thing each day that feels a bit challenging. Over time, each success builds confidence.
- **Surrounding Them with Kindness**: Ask teachers, relatives, or neighbors to speak positively with them. Negative self-image can change if children see that people around them notice their worth.

Link Between Self-Worth, Resilience, and Kindness
When children have a healthy sense of worth and resilience, they often treat others with respect. They do not feel the need to bully or belittle because they already feel valued. Their resilience helps them handle conflicts without lashing out. As a result, they become examples for others, showing that you can be strong and kind at the same time. This cycle encourages more caring interactions in schools and communities, because children see that self-confidence and empathy can go hand in hand.

Looking to the Future
Self-worth and resilience are not traits children either have or do not have. They are skills that grow over time with the right support. Each time a child overcomes a setback or takes pride in something they have learned, these qualities grow a little more. Adults can nurture them by believing in the child's potential, guiding them with patience, and celebrating small steps of progress (all while avoiding harmful words that magnify mistakes).

Building self-worth and resilience benefits everyone. It means fewer children turning to bullying to feel strong, more children standing up for what is right, and communities becoming safer and friendlier. When children trust in their abilities, they are ready to face life's hurdles without causing harm. They can keep learning, stand up for themselves and others, and recover from failures with hope for the future.

In the end, a community full of resilient children with healthy self-worth is a place where bullying finds little room to grow. People are more likely to help each other, solve conflicts calmly, and appreciate what each person brings. By focusing on these qualities—both in the classroom and at home—we shape a world where children grow up confident, caring, and ready to face the ups and downs of life with open hearts and minds.

Chapter 13: Handling Conflict and Anger

Conflict is a normal part of life. People have different views, feelings, and needs, so they do not always agree. While conflict itself is not always harmful, the way people handle it can either help them grow or cause trouble. One reason bullying happens is that some people cope with anger or frustration by hurting others. If children and teens learn healthier ways to handle conflict and anger, they are less likely to turn to bullying. In this chapter, we will discuss why conflicts arise, how anger can lead to bullying, and methods that help both children and adults manage these strong emotions in a safer way.

---

1. **What Causes Conflict?**
   Conflict often happens when people want different things or misunderstand each other. In schools, small disagreements can start over group projects, seating in the cafeteria, or sports teams. At home, arguments can arise over chores, bedtime, or who gets control of the TV. In friendships, conflict might begin when someone feels left out or believes a friend is ignoring them. These moments become dangerous if anger takes over and there is no respectful way to fix the disagreement.

Not every conflict leads to bullying. If both sides have the same power level and can express themselves calmly, it might be resolved in a fair way. However, when someone tries to dominate or refuses to respect the other person's views, conflict can become unhealthy. Repeated or aggressive behavior could then turn into bullying, where one side regularly intimidates or harms the other.

2. **Why Anger Can Escalate Conflicts**
   Anger is a normal emotion that warns us something is wrong. We might feel angry if we think someone is treating us unfairly, or if we are stressed and cannot find relief. But when anger becomes too strong, it can shut down our ability to think clearly. We might say cruel words or lash out physically, which only adds to the tension.

Children who feel anger but lack skills to handle it might use bullying as an outlet. They could push a classmate, shout insults, or spread rumors to feel some sense of control. Others might become angry bystanders, watching someone else bully a target without stepping in. This anger can also come from problems in their own lives. Maybe they are upset about a family situation or worried about grades. If they do not know how to manage these feelings, they might take them out on peers.

3. **Recognizing Signs of Conflict and Anger**
   It helps to spot conflict early. Signs could include a tense atmosphere, an exchange of insults, or even silent looks of disapproval between classmates. If a situation is growing tense, someone might clench their fists or raise their voice. They might glare or roll their eyes in frustration. Anger signs can include a red face, a trembling voice, or a sudden shift in tone. Once these signs appear, the chance of bullying can increase if the conflict is not addressed.

In group settings, adults can look for subtle clues. If a group of children suddenly goes quiet when a certain person enters, or if the atmosphere feels charged with hostility, there may be unspoken conflict. Spotting these moments allows adults to gently ask questions and calm things down before anger erupts.

Teaching Children to Identify Their Feelings

A big part of handling conflict and anger is recognizing emotions before they spiral out of control. Children often feel anger in their bodies. Their hearts might beat faster, or their muscles might tighten. They may start to breathe heavily. Teaching them to notice these signs can help them take a pause before they do or say something hurtful.

Adults can use short exercises to help. For instance, they can ask children to close their eyes and think about how their body feels when they are relaxed versus when they are angry. They can mention where they might feel heat or tension. By naming these feelings—"My heart is racing," "My stomach feels tight"—the child can learn to see anger as a signal, not an automatic reason to lash out.

Healthy Ways to Express Anger

Anger is not bad by itself. It can even be helpful when it alerts us that something is unfair. The key is to express anger in ways that do not harm others. Some positive approaches include:

Talking: Finding a safe person to talk with about what is upsetting, whether that is a friend, teacher, or counselor.

Writing or Drawing: Putting anger into words on paper or sketching how it feels can release tension.

- **Physical Outlets**: Exercise like running or playing sports can burn off the energy caused by anger.
- **Calming Techniques**: Simple steps such as deep breathing, counting to ten, or stepping away from the argument can help the body and mind cool down.

By learning these strategies, children do not have to rely on bullying or meanness to release anger.

Conflict Resolution Steps

When conflict arises, using a clear process can prevent it from turning into bullying. A common method includes:

- **Calm Down**: All sides take a moment to breathe or step away. This keeps anger from controlling the conversation.
- **Listen**: Each person shares their view without interruptions. Listening helps people realize they may have misunderstood each other.
- **Repeat**: Each side repeats the other's main points to show they heard correctly.
- **Find Common Ground**: Look for areas of agreement or shared goals.
- **Discuss Solutions**: Brainstorm ways to solve the issue. The solution should respect everyone involved.
- **Agree and Plan**: Choose a solution and decide the next steps or rules for the future.

Schools, families, and youth programs can teach this method through practice. Younger children might role-play, acting out typical conflicts and using these steps to resolve them. Over time, it becomes a habit.

Supporting Children Who Struggle with Anger

Some children need extra help if they show ongoing anger problems. This might include therapy, counseling, or anger management sessions. A counselor can teach them how to recognize early signals of frustration and guide them toward better coping methods. If there are deep-rooted issues, such as stress at home, the counselor might help the entire family find solutions.

Teachers and parents can also work together. If a child often has angry outbursts at school, the teacher could keep a close eye on triggers—maybe certain group activities or competitive games cause the child's anger to spike. By adjusting tasks or seating arrangements, adults can reduce the chance of conflict.

Modeling Calm Behavior

Children watch adults all the time, picking up cues on how to act. If they see parents or teachers yelling, slamming doors, or using harsh words whenever conflict happens, they might think that is normal. If they see calm discussion, respectful debate, or apologies from adults, they learn that it is possible to handle conflict without aggression.

Adults can model calm behavior by:

- **Taking a breath when upset**: Saying out loud, "I'm feeling angry, so I'm going to count to ten before I respond."
- **Using respectful words**: Even in frustration, avoiding insults and name-calling.
- **Apologizing**: If an adult overreacts, they can say, "I'm sorry I raised my voice. That was not the right way to handle it."

This approach shows children that everyone gets angry, but we can still handle it in a caring way.

Group Norms for Conflict

In schools or clubs, setting group norms can prevent bullying. Norms can include:

- **"We treat each other with respect."**
- **"We keep our voices calm when we disagree."**
- **"We do not interrupt when someone else is talking."**
- **"We look for win-win solutions."**

If these guidelines are repeated often and enforced fairly, children learn that aggressive or mean behavior is not acceptable. Over time, these norms become part of the group's culture, making bullying less likely.

Using Empathy to Defuse Anger

Empathy is powerful in calming conflicts. If children learn to pause and consider the other person's feelings, they might realize the other side is also upset or scared. Instead of jumping to insults, they can say something like, "I can see you're upset—what's wrong?" This simple step can lower tension and open the door to conversation rather than fighting.

Empathy does not mean giving in to unfair demands. It just means recognizing the other person's emotions. When people feel heard, they are less likely to escalate the conflict into bullying or name-calling.

Anger and the Bystander's Role
Bystanders can also help when anger flares. They can gently urge the two sides to calm down before things get worse. For instance, a friend might say, "Let's sit for a minute and breathe," or "Let's talk one at a time." They might invite the pair to follow a conflict resolution process. If bystanders remain silent while tensions rise, the chance of bullying grows.

Adults who witness conflict can do the same. Rather than shouting, they might step between the two sides and ask them to lower their voices, then guide them through a short discussion. If the situation is too heated, separating them temporarily can prevent immediate harm. Once they have cooled off, the adult can help them talk things out.

When Conflict Becomes Bullying
Sometimes, a conflict turns into a pattern where one person targets another repeatedly. At this point, it is no longer just a disagreement. It becomes bullying, and stronger intervention may be needed. This could involve:

- **Documenting the behavior**: Writing down when and how it happens.
- **Contacting parents or guardians**: Letting them know what is going on and asking for their cooperation.
- **Involving school authorities**: Counselors or principals can step in if the bullying happens at school.
- **Seeking professional help**: If the bully's anger is extreme or if the target's well-being is at risk, therapy or mediation may be necessary.

Ignoring repeated aggression might send a signal that bullying is allowed. So, it is important to act quickly when a conflict crosses this line.

Special Cases: Cyber Anger
Anger can also show up online. People might send rude or threatening messages or post nasty comments when they are upset. Because there is no face-to-face

contact, it can be easier to say cruel things. Children (and adults) need guidance on handling online anger. A few tips include:

- **Cooling Down Before Replying**: If someone writes an upsetting comment, taking time to calm down before responding can prevent a mean reply.
- **Avoiding Group Piles**: Sometimes, a group of online friends might gang up on one person, teasing or mocking them. Urge children not to join in.
- **Reporting**: If a conversation becomes hostile, children should be encouraged to block the person and report the behavior to the platform.
- **Privacy Control**: Keeping profiles private and limiting contact with strangers can reduce heated or harmful exchanges.

Teaching Coping Skills Early
The sooner children learn to handle anger and conflicts, the more natural these skills become. Even preschoolers can learn simple ways to say, "I don't like that," or to breathe when they feel upset. As they grow older, they can practice more advanced steps like using "I" statements—"I feel upset when you grab my toy because it makes me feel ignored." Starting young prevents a lot of tension later on.

Handling Strong Feelings in Groups
Sometimes, an entire group might be tense or angry, maybe because they lost an important game or because they are stressed about upcoming exams. In these cases, the group might blame one person or lash out. A teacher, coach, or group leader can help by calling a quick meeting to let everyone talk about their feelings. Letting them voice frustrations can prevent them from picking a scapegoat. This kind of group talk should be guided, ensuring the tone stays respectful.

Apologizing and Repairing Relationships
Conflict can bruise relationships. Apologies help fix that. Teaching children to give a real apology goes beyond saying, "I'm sorry." It involves acknowledging what happened, showing regret for the harm, and possibly making amends. For example, if a child broke another's art project in anger, they might offer to help fix it or create a new one together. When apologies are sincere, trust can begin to rebuild. This shows children that conflict does not have to lead to lasting damage.

When to Seek Extra Help

Sometimes, conflicts keep popping up no matter what. The same child might keep losing their temper, or the same group might keep having blowups. At that point, deeper issues might be at play—maybe there is a hidden problem at home, a mental health issue, or a lack of adult oversight. Schools or families should consider:

- **Counseling**: A professional can help uncover triggers for constant anger and suggest coping strategies.
- **Mentoring**: An older student or caring adult could guide the child in practicing conflict resolution.
- **Family Intervention**: If home stress is fueling the child's anger, the entire family may benefit from talking with a counselor about healthy communication.

Early help can prevent patterns of anger from solidifying.

Cultural Differences in Handling Conflict

Families and communities have different ways of dealing with conflict. Some prefer open discussions, while others discourage direct confrontation. It is important to honor these differences but also ensure that children learn respectful ways to manage anger. If a child's family style is very strict, they might fear speaking up, which can cause frustration that explodes later. On the other hand, a family that encourages endless arguing might need to teach children to calm down and take turns listening. Understanding cultural norms can help parents, teachers, and counselors provide guidance that fits the child's background.

Benefits of Healthy Conflict Handling

When children learn to handle conflict and anger well:

- **They Form Stronger Friendships**: People trust them not to lash out.
- **They Avoid Bullying**: They do not need to belittle others to feel in control.
- **They Become Better Problem-Solvers**: They look for logical solutions rather than shouting or threatening.
- **They Grow Emotional Strength**: Each conflict they manage well boosts their confidence that they can handle tough moments.

Over time, these skills help them succeed in school, work, and family life. They also contribute to safer, happier communities because fewer disagreements turn into aggression.

Looking Ahead
Conflict and anger do not have to be scary. They can be signals that something needs attention. If children learn to handle these feelings thoughtfully, they are less likely to let them turn into bullying. They can even use conflict to understand themselves and others better. Schools, families, and communities all have a role in guiding children toward calmer, kinder ways of dealing with tension.

By offering clear steps, modeling calm behavior, and teaching empathy, adults can help children see that anger can be managed in a respectful way. This knowledge not only decreases bullying but also lays a foundation for healthy relationships throughout life. People who grow up with these skills are more likely to talk through problems, compromise, and find peaceful solutions. In this way, handling conflict and anger is not just about stopping bullying—it is about building the emotional strength and respect that let everyone thrive.

Chapter 14: Changing Group Behavior

Bullying is often not just about two people. Sometimes, entire groups of classmates, teammates, or friends play a part, whether by supporting the bully, laughing along, or standing silent. Changing group behavior can make a huge difference in stopping bullying. When a group decides it does not accept cruelty or meanness, the bully's power shrinks. In this chapter, we will explore how group behaviors form, why groups might allow or encourage bullying, and how to guide groups to be more welcoming and respectful.

---

1. **How Groups Affect Behavior**
   When people gather in groups, they often follow unspoken rules about what is allowed. This is sometimes called "group culture." For example, if a popular student at school mocks someone, others may laugh just to fit in. If a group of friends always uses mean jokes, a new member might join in because they think that is the normal way to behave. At sports practice, a powerful player might haze younger players, and teammates who do not want to be targeted next stay quiet.

These group rules can become so strong that individuals go against their own sense of kindness. They might bully because everyone else is doing it, or because they fear they will be picked on if they stand out. On the flip side, groups can also encourage positive actions. If the most well-liked students stand up for kindness, others may follow that example. That is why targeting the entire group's norms is key to cutting down bullying.

Recognizing Group Influence in Bullying
Group bullying can look like:

- **A Group Teasing One Person**: Instead of one bully, several friends take part in mocking someone.
- **Rumor Chains**: Someone spreads a rumor, and others pass it along to stay in the group's favor.
- **Exclusion**: A group decides who is "in" and who is "out," leaving one person friendless and isolated.
- **Encouraging Harm**: A crowd circles around to watch a fight or laughs while someone is teased.

When the group acts together, the target faces more than just one bully—they face the weight of many people who seem united against them. This can feel extremely scary.

Why Groups Might Support a Bully
A few factors can cause a group to back a bully:

- **Fear**: People worry they will be the next victim if they do not join in.
- **Belonging**: Some group members think that agreeing with the bully helps them fit in.
- **Admiration**: If the bully is seen as popular or strong, people might follow them for social advantage.
- **Lack of Awareness**: Some do not realize the harm they cause by laughing at mean jokes or gossip.

Understanding these reasons helps parents, teachers, and counselors see why certain group members do not speak up. Often, they do not want trouble, so they choose silence or go along with the bully.

Shifting the Group Mindset
Changing group behavior means teaching everyone that kindness is the new normal. This can happen when leaders in the group—popular kids, older siblings, team captains—show that bullying is not welcome. If a star athlete says, "Let's not tease him; it's not cool," others might follow suit. If a class president posts messages against bullying on social media, classmates may start viewing it as something worth speaking out against.

Teachers, parents, or coaches can also talk directly to the group about their roles. For instance, a coach might say, "On this team, we respect everyone. If you see someone being mistreated, step in or tell me." By stating clear expectations, adults invite the whole group to adopt a culture of respect.

Group Activities That Build Team Spirit
Sometimes groups bully because they lack genuine connection. They have no real sense of friendship beyond picking on others. Activities that strengthen bonds in a positive way can shift this dynamic:

- **Team Challenges**: Group puzzles or tasks that require every member to work together can foster respect.

- **Goal Setting**: If a class or club sets a shared goal—like collecting items for a local drive—they learn to support each other for a good cause.
- **Praise for Cooperation**: Recognize moments when the group helps each other instead of mocking or excluding. This positive feedback shows the benefits of kindness.
- **Small Group Talks**: In a class or youth group, splitting into smaller circles to discuss how bullying feels can build empathy. Hearing real experiences can open eyes to the harm done by group cruelty.

Empowering Bystanders

A bystander is someone who sees bullying but is not directly involved as the main bully or the main target. In groups, bystanders can be very powerful. If enough bystanders refuse to laugh or encourage the bully, the bullying might stop. Adults can encourage this by:

- **Teaching Safe Responses**: Bystanders can quietly say, "That's not funny," or "Let's leave him alone," or even walk away to show disapproval.
- **Reporting**: If the group is too scary, telling an adult is an important step. This is not tattling—it is preventing harm.
- **Offering Support to the Target**: A bystander might say, "I'm sorry they did that to you," or invite the target to sit with them. This reduces the target's isolation.

When bystanders realize they can act without being a bully themselves, they may feel stronger. Each small action chips away at the bully's control.

Leaders Who Influence Groups

Groups often have one or more leaders—people who shape the group's actions, whether intentionally or not. A leader might be popular because of looks, skills, or confidence. If this leader is the bully, they can spread meanness. But if the leader is kind, they can discourage meanness quickly. Adults can ask positive leaders to help set a better tone. For example, a teacher might say to a well-liked student, "Others look up to you. Could you help me make sure everyone feels included?"

When a leader stands up to bullying, it sends a message that cruelty is not admired. This often has a bigger impact than rules alone because peers see that kindness can be cool, too.

Changing Online Group Behavior

Groups also form online, in chat groups or social media circles. Bullying might involve sharing cruel memes, leaving mean comments, or mocking someone in a group chat. To change online group behavior:

- **Set Posting Guidelines**: Groups can agree not to post rude comments or share personal information without permission.
- **Encourage Reporting**: Remind children they can report abusive content to the platform or a trusted adult.
- **Promote Positive Challenges**: Instead of "roasting" someone, groups can do friendly challenges, share uplifting posts, or highlight each other's achievements.
- **Call Out Hurtful Behavior**: If someone shares a cruel post, a group member can reply, "That's not right—please remove it." Just one voice can change the tone.

Stopping "In" and "Out" Groups

Bullying sometimes revolves around labeling a certain set of people as "cool" and another as "uncool." The "in" group then harasses anyone who does not fit their standards. This might be based on looks, interests, or family background. To reduce this:

- **Mixing Activities**: Arrange events where students from different social circles work together. When they cooperate, they see each other as real people, not stereotypes.
- **Highlighting Unique Strengths**: Teachers or coaches can point out each student's positive traits so no group believes they are the only ones who matter.
- **Encouraging Friendships Across Groups**: Clubs, sports, or arts programs that include a variety of students can break down walls.
- **Standing Against Name-Calling**: Words like "loser" or "weirdo" can become normal in certain groups. Stopping these terms can help.

When Groups Spread Rumors

Rumors and gossip can spread quickly in a group. It might start with a small lie or an exaggeration, but if the group keeps repeating it, the target can be hurt or shamed. Teachers or parents might:

- **Explain the Harm of Rumors**: Show how spreading unverified claims can damage someone's reputation.
- **Encourage Fact-Checking**: Teach children to ask, "Where did you hear that?" and "Is that really true?" before passing it on.
- **Talk About Accountability**: Remind children that just passing the rumor along still causes harm.
- **Provide Truthful Info**: If the rumor is about something personal, the target can choose to set the record straight if they feel comfortable. Adults can also help correct false information in a calm manner.

Peer Mediation for Groups

Some schools use peer mediation programs where trained students help classmates discuss problems. This is especially helpful for group conflicts. Mediators guide them to see each other's points of view and find a solution that works for everyone. Because the mediators are peers, group members might feel less defensive than if a teacher or principal steps in. This approach can reveal hidden reasons behind bullying, such as jealousy or competition. After mediation, groups may adopt new norms that reduce future conflict.

Adjusting Group Leadership Roles

In some groups, the official leader or captain might misuse their power. Reassigning roles or rotating leadership can show that power is shared. For example:

- **Rotating Captainship**: In a sports team, let each member be captain for a week.
- **Team Votes**: If a group project needs a leader, let the team vote or take turns, so no one person always holds control.
- **Teacher-Selected Leaders**: A teacher might pick students who show kindness or fairness to be in charge of certain tasks, rather than those who are just outspoken.

Spreading responsibility discourages a single bully from dominating. It also helps quieter members practice leadership in a supportive setting.

Rewards for Positive Group Behavior

When a group shows signs of improvement—like including others or standing up for a target—adults can praise them in front of others. Small acknowledgments, such as a kind note or a quick announcement during class, can reinforce that the group's good actions matter. Some schools set up a point system where classes earn points for positive behavior. At the end of the week or month, they might get a simple reward (such as extra free time) if they keep up the respectful attitude. This approach should not be overused, but it can motivate groups to keep treating people well.

Correcting Group Misconduct
When a group crosses a line and bullies someone, consequences must be consistent and fair. Adults can:

- **Speak to Them as a Group**: Explain clearly why their actions are harmful and not allowed.
- **Separate Key Instigators**: If one or two students are fueling the bullying, removing them from the group activity can reduce the problem.
- **Require Restorative Actions**: They might apologize, help the target in some way, or engage in a reflective assignment about kindness.
- **Contact Parents**: Group bullying can be serious, so letting all parents know the situation might encourage discussions at home.

The goal is not to just punish, but to make sure the group understands the impact of their actions and commits to change.

Tackling Cliques
Cliques are small, closed-off groups that decide who can join and who cannot. They can lead to bullying by shutting out people or teasing those who do not fit. Teachers and youth leaders can address cliques by:

- **Mixing Up Groups Regularly**: During class or events, assign mixed teams so the same small cluster of friends does not always stay together.
- **Emphasizing Inclusion**: Provide seating or group activities that encourage people to learn about classmates outside their usual circle.
- **Teaching Friendship Skills**: Help children practice how to invite a new person to sit with them or join a game.
- **Watching for Exclusion**: If certain kids are always left alone, talk with the clique about the effects of leaving people out.

Community Support for Group Change
Sometimes, groups form outside school—like neighborhood kids, faith-based youth groups, or sports teams in the community. Coaches, community center staff, and other adults can help by:

- **Hosting Workshops**: Invite a local expert to discuss bullying, respect, and teamwork.
- **Monitoring Gatherings**: Make sure there are enough adults around to notice group bullying behaviors.
- **Setting Shared Standards**: Post rules about kindness in community spaces so everyone knows how they should behave.
- **Encouraging Mentorship**: Pair older teens with younger ones to create supportive bonds that reduce cliques and encourage empathy.

Long-Term Effects of Group Change
When a group decides to adopt a kinder culture, it can have lasting effects:

- **Less Fear**: Members do not worry about being shamed or mocked for expressing their thoughts.
- **Improved Confidence**: People feel safer to try new things or share new ideas.
- **Better Problem-Solving**: With less hostility, groups can focus on goals or activities rather than dealing with tension.
- **Positive Ripple**: Other groups see that it is possible to thrive without bullying, and they might adopt similar changes.

Young people who experience a respectful group environment gain skills they can use in other parts of life, such as future workplaces or family relationships.

Handling Resistance
Not every group member will welcome change. Some might enjoy the power they get from bullying or see no reason to be more inclusive. To handle this:

- **Stay Firm on Rules**: Consistency is key. Do not let a few people break the new norms without consequences.
- **Offer Guidance**: If a student resists, talk with them privately to find out why. Maybe they fear losing status or they have personal troubles. Offer support where possible.
- **Show Benefits**: Point out how the group is happier or more successful when people cooperate.
- **Seek Backup**: If troublemakers continue, get help from principals, parents, or coaches who can reinforce that bullying is not allowed.

Putting the Target in the Group
Sometimes, the bullied person feels they cannot ever join the group.

Encouraging the group to welcome them can help repair harm. Activities that require team cooperation, supervised by an adult, can ease this transition. The group can learn that the target has ideas and strengths, and the target can see not everyone wants to harm them. Over time, a respectful environment can help them feel more comfortable. This process takes patience, and the target should never be forced to join if they are not ready. The goal is to offer a chance for inclusion once the group's norms have changed.

Looking to the Future
Changing a group's behavior is a powerful way to reduce bullying. While individual interventions do matter, addressing the whole group creates lasting effects. When classmates, teams, or friends learn to stand up for kindness, bullying becomes less appealing. People see they do not need to tear others down to bond. Instead, they discover that supporting each other can create a stronger sense of belonging than fear ever could.

Groups influence how children and teens see themselves and others. By guiding these groups toward respectful norms, we help everyone grow. The child who was once a bystander can become a confident helper, the bully can learn new ways to connect, and the target can feel safe. Over time, this approach shapes schools, communities, and online spaces into places where meanness does not thrive. It also teaches young people the value of working together in a positive way—a skill that will serve them for their entire lives.

Chapter 15: Legal and Policy Perspectives

Bullying is not just a personal or social problem—it is also an issue that many governments, school districts, and institutions address through laws and policies. These legal and policy measures help set standards for how schools and communities should prevent and respond to bullying. They also clarify what consequences might follow if someone breaks the rules. By having clear policies and, in some cases, legal consequences, society sends a firm message that bullying is taken seriously. In this chapter, we will look at the ways legal and policy perspectives aim to reduce bullying and safeguard the rights of everyone involved.

---

1. **The Reason for Laws and Policies**
   Laws and policies exist so that everyone has a clear understanding of what behavior is allowed and what is not. If a child or teenager is bullied, they need to know that adults have a plan to protect them. If someone is tempted to bully, they should realize that there could be penalties, such as suspension from school or legal consequences if the bullying is severe. For school officials and community leaders, policies provide a roadmap for how to handle reports of bullying. Without these guidelines, responses can be random or unfair.

Legal measures also help create an environment where targets feel comfortable speaking up. Sometimes, children fear that if they complain about a bully, nothing will change or they might face worse harassment. But when the school or the law stands firmly on the side of safety and respect, it becomes easier for targets to come forward. In the big picture, having formal rules encourages everyone to treat each other with respect, reminding us that safety and dignity are essential rights for all people.

2. **School Policies on Bullying**
   Many schools have codes of conduct that outline acceptable and unacceptable behavior. These documents often define bullying, stating that repeated actions aimed at harming or intimidating a student are not allowed. Some school policies also list specific steps to take if bullying is reported. For example, they might require teachers to file a written

report, meet with both the bully and the target, and notify parents. This approach ensures that the school responds quickly and consistently.

Some school policies also include training sessions for teachers and staff, showing them how to identify signs of bullying and intervene effectively. A teacher might learn how to separate students involved in a conflict calmly or how to document incidents so that a pattern of bullying can be spotted. In some places, the policy also mandates that schools teach students about empathy, kindness, and problem-solving skills. By adding these lessons into the curriculum, schools aim to reduce bullying before it starts.

3. **State or Regional Laws**

   In many regions, there are laws requiring schools to have anti-bullying programs. These laws may require schools to keep records of bullying reports, investigate complaints, and ensure that those who bully face consequences. The laws might also require parents to be informed of serious incidents. In some places, schools that fail to follow these procedures could face government penalties. This encourages school administrators to pay close attention to bullying and not overlook it.

These state or regional laws can also set the basic definition of bullying. For example, the law might say that bullying involves a power imbalance and repeated harm. By defining bullying carefully, the law clarifies that this is not just a one-time argument between equals. If the bullying includes threats, bodily harm, or extreme harassment, it can rise to the level of criminal behavior under other laws as well.

4. **Cyberbullying and the Law**

   With the rise of technology, cyberbullying has become a major concern. In some regions, new laws or updates to existing ones cover bullying that occurs through electronic devices. A state might require schools to treat cyberbullying the same way as face-to-face bullying if it affects a student's ability to learn or feel safe at school. Laws might also empower schools to discipline students for cyberbullying that happens off campus if the behavior creates a hostile environment for the target.

In some severe cases, cyberbullying can violate harassment or stalking laws. If someone sends repeated threats or shares private information to ruin a target's reputation, the bully might be investigated by the police. Of course, not every act of online teasing leads to criminal charges. Usually, law enforcement gets involved if the behavior is especially serious or if a restraining order is needed to protect the target.

5. **Federal Protections in Certain Countries**
   In some nations, there are national or federal laws that protect individuals from harassment, especially if the bullying is linked to discrimination based on race, gender, disability, or other protected characteristics. For instance, if a student is bullied because of their religion, this could violate federal civil rights laws in certain places. In these cases, government agencies might investigate the school to see if they failed to protect the bullied student. If so, the school might be required to take corrective measures, such as improving staff training, adjusting policies, or paying fines.

For families of bullied students, knowing that broader legal protections exist can be comforting. It reassures them that the law recognizes their right to learn in a safe environment and that the government can step in if schools do not act. These federal protections also underline a moral and legal stance that harassment tied to prejudice is not tolerated.

6. **Reporting Mechanisms**
   Legal and policy measures often include details on how a target or witness can report bullying. In many schools, a student can tell a teacher or counselor, who is then required to pass the information on to the principal. Some schools provide an anonymous tip line or drop box so that students can report bullying without fear of being identified. This can be important if the child worries about retaliation.

Reporting does not guarantee that bullying stops instantly, but it starts a process. The school typically investigates the claim, interviews those involved, and checks any evidence, such as witness statements or text messages. If they confirm bullying took place, they follow the disciplinary actions stated in the policy. Depending on the severity, consequences can range from warnings or detentions to suspensions or expulsions. In very serious cases, or if a crime was committed, law enforcement may become involved.

7. **School Liability and Lawsuits**
   Another reason schools take bullying policies seriously is the risk of legal

liability. Families might sue a school if they believe the school did not protect their child from repeated harm. For instance, if a child was severely bullied multiple times, and the school had been informed but failed to act, parents might argue that the school neglected its duty. In some lawsuits, courts have awarded financial damages to families, adding more pressure on schools to enforce anti-bullying measures.

At the same time, not every case of bullying ends up in court. Going through a lawsuit can be time-consuming and expensive, and families typically prefer that the school fixes the situation rather than having to sue. However, the possibility of legal action pushes schools to keep strong records of how they respond to bullying reports. This can include notes from meetings with students, copies of relevant emails, and logs of phone calls with parents. If they show a genuine effort to address bullying, schools are less likely to face legal problems.

8. **Policies for Teachers and Staff**
   Teachers and school staff can also be subject to policies and laws concerning bullying. For instance, if a staff member bullies a student (through harsh language, threats, or unfair treatment), that could lead to professional discipline or termination. Some places have laws covering abuse of power by teachers, and these laws protect students' rights.

In addition, policies often require teachers to report bullying they witness. If a teacher turns a blind eye or ignores the situation, they could face consequences. Training programs try to ensure that all staff—teachers, cafeteria workers, bus drivers—know how to spot and intervene in bullying situations. This broad approach is crucial, because bullying can happen anywhere on campus or on the ride to and from school.

9. **Restorative Approaches in Policies**
   While some policies focus on punishment, others emphasize restorative practices. Restorative approaches aim to help both the bully and the target move forward in a healthier way. Instead of just suspending the bully, for example, a policy might require a restorative conference. This involves the bully, the target, and sometimes parents or counselors sitting down with a trained facilitator. They discuss the harm done, the reasons behind the behavior, and possible ways to repair the relationship.

In these sessions, the bully is encouraged to take responsibility for their actions. The target can share how the bullying made them feel. Together, they might agree on steps such as an apology, community service, or continued counseling. Restorative methods have gained popularity because they can lower the chance of repeat bullying and help the bully change long-term behavior rather than just receiving a short-term punishment.

10. **Balancing Discipline and Education**
    A challenge for many schools is striking the right balance between discipline and learning. If policies are too harsh, a child who bullies might feel resentful and refuse to improve. If policies are too soft, targets might feel unsafe. Ideally, policies give administrators enough flexibility to adapt discipline to each situation. For a first offense involving mild bullying, a meeting and a warning might be enough. But if bullying is extreme or repeated, stricter measures become necessary.

Many schools also incorporate educational steps. A bully might attend counseling sessions on anger management or empathy training to understand the effects of their actions. The goal is not just to punish but to guide the bully toward healthier interactions. Policies that include these educational components often see better results, because the root causes of bullying—such as low self-esteem, trouble at home, or lack of social skills—are being addressed, not just the symptoms.

11. **Policies for Special Cases**
    Some children have specific needs or disabilities that can put them at risk of being bullied or might lead them to bully unintentionally. For example, a child with autism might struggle to read social cues and accidentally say things that upset peers. A child with ADHD might have outbursts that anger classmates, which can trigger conflict. Policies sometimes mention the need for extra support in these cases. Schools might provide an aide, create a behavior plan, or adjust the environment so that stress for the student is minimized.

Likewise, if a student is bullied because of a disability, the school may have extra legal duties to ensure the child's right to a free and appropriate education in a safe environment. In some places, ignoring such bullying could be considered a violation of disability rights, leading to legal or financial penalties for the school district.

12. **The Role of Parents and Guardians**
    Laws and policies often include parents in the process. Schools might require a meeting with the parents of both the bully and the target, giving them a chance to hear the evidence and share their perspectives. Policies might encourage parents to seek counseling for their child if the bullying is serious. If parents refuse to cooperate, the school can still move forward with disciplinary steps, but good parental involvement can speed up a resolution.

In some regions, parents can face legal consequences if they knowingly allow their child to bully others or if they harass the target themselves. This is more common in severe cases, but it does highlight that parents also have a responsibility to guide their child away from harmful behavior. When parents work with the school to enforce boundaries and teach empathy, the child is more likely to change.

13. **Community-Level Policies**
    Beyond schools, community centers, sports leagues, and other youth organizations can have their own policies. These might specify that members who bully other participants will be removed from the program. Coaches, volunteers, and staff often receive training on how to notice and address bullying or hazing. Although these community policies are not always backed by the same legal force as school or state rules, they still matter. They show that the entire community stands against bullying, not just the school.

Sometimes, local governments or city councils might pass ordinances encouraging businesses, libraries, and sports clubs to have clear anti-bullying guidelines. These ordinances might not carry large fines, but they help spread the message that bullying is everyone's concern. They also encourage sharing of resources, like training materials or conflict resolution programs, among different groups in the community.

14. **Challenges in Enforcing Policies**
    Despite clear rules and laws, enforcing anti-bullying measures can be tricky. Some students might hide their bullying behavior, doing it online or in places with no adult supervision. Others might bully in subtle ways, like spreading rumors or excluding someone from a group, making it hard

to prove. School staff might feel overwhelmed if they have large classes or limited time to monitor halls and lunch areas.

It can also be challenging if the bully has strong social power. Some bystanders or even adults might be reluctant to speak against a well-liked student or an influential family. In other cases, staff might not fully believe the target's complaints, especially if the bullying is psychological. Nonetheless, policies strive to address these problems by spelling out the duty of teachers to investigate carefully, protect the target, and keep records even of smaller incidents. Over time, patterns can emerge, revealing that the same student is causing harm repeatedly.

15. **Improving Policies Over Time**
    As more research is done and more stories about bullying come to light, policies evolve. Some schools update their codes to include detailed cyberbullying sections. Others expand definitions of bullying to make sure no one slips through the cracks. Parent groups, student councils, and community leaders often join in discussions to help shape these updates. By sharing success stories and challenges, schools learn from each other and improve their anti-bullying approaches.

In some areas, schools consult with mental health professionals to create policies that recognize how trauma, stress, or mental disorders might fuel bullying. Instead of focusing only on punishment, these policies guide schools to offer counseling, conflict resolution, and skill-building workshops. Families, too, might attend sessions to learn how to support positive changes at home.

16. **Seeing Laws and Policies as Part of a Bigger Plan**
    Legal and policy perspectives on bullying are crucial, but they are not the sole solution. These rules create a framework that demands accountability, but preventing bullying also requires kindness, empathy, and strong relationships. Laws might stop some bullies out of fear of punishment. Policies might hold schools or organizations responsible. Yet the deeper change often comes from teaching values that support respect, from early childhood onward.

When laws and policies are combined with empathy lessons, parental involvement, and community support, the impact can be powerful. Targets feel safer to speak up, bystanders know how to help, and bullies learn that their actions have real consequences. Over time, as more people understand the seriousness of bullying and how to prevent it, society can move closer to environments where every child feels safe to learn, play, and grow.

17. **Empowering Students with Knowledge of Their Rights**
    One positive aspect of clear policies is that students can learn their own rights. If they experience bullying, they know they can report it and expect the school to act. Students also discover that they can raise concerns with a counselor, teacher, or even an external agency if the school does not respond. This knowledge reduces a sense of helplessness. It shows them that they have options and that bullying is not something they have to endure in silence.

In some schools, student councils or clubs create brochures or hold assemblies to explain the policy in simple terms. They might clarify who to talk to, how to keep evidence of bullying, and what to expect after a report. This transparency helps keep the policy from being just words on paper. It becomes a living guide that students can rely on.

18. **Critiques and Ongoing Debates**
    Not everyone agrees on how strict or broad anti-bullying laws and policies should be. Some worry that too many rules make children overly cautious, stifling normal childhood interactions. Others argue that certain policies do not go far enough to protect targets of severe bullying. There might be debates about whether certain forms of teasing or rough play count as bullying, or if an action was "just a joke." These debates can shape how policies are written and enforced.

Another concern is that schools might focus on punishing bullies without helping them change. Critics say that policies should go beyond discipline to include counseling, support groups, and family interventions. Others worry about free speech rights, especially in cases of online conflicts. Balancing all these interests can be challenging, and lawmakers often revisit anti-bullying legislation to refine it.

19. **How to Use Policies Effectively**
    For policies to work, schools need to communicate them clearly. Teachers and staff should know exactly what steps to follow when they see or hear about bullying. Parents need to be informed about the policy so they can

support it at home. Students should learn about it in simple language, through lessons or assemblies. When everyone knows the rules and how to report problems, the policy becomes a tool for positive change, not just a formality.

Families can also do their part by keeping records of bullying incidents—dates, times, descriptions—so that if they need to meet with school officials, they have clear information. They can calmly reference the policy to show which parts they believe were not followed. This approach helps hold the school accountable without turning the meeting into a shouting match. In the best-case scenario, staff and parents work together to solve the problem and prevent more harm.

20. **Looking Forward**

    Legal and policy perspectives on bullying continue to evolve as society learns more about the emotional damage it causes. The hope is that as policies strengthen, fewer students will feel alone or unsafe, and fewer bullies will believe they can act without consequences. Yet the goal is not only to prevent legal trouble. It is to foster communities where children grow up with empathy, respect, and the freedom to pursue their interests without fear.

By understanding these rules, families, educators, and students can use them to create safer schools and neighborhoods. Combined with personal growth, empathy, and community-wide efforts, strong laws and policies help ensure that bullying remains unacceptable. Although they are just one part of the solution, they are a key factor in shaping an environment where everyone's rights are upheld. In the next chapters, we will explore more ways that bullying can be addressed at home, in schools, and in the broader community—further connecting these policy frameworks with real-life action and change.

Chapter 16: Addressing Bullying at Home

Home is often where children first learn how to communicate, solve disputes, and treat others. It is also where children should feel the safest. However, bullying can touch family life in different ways. A child might come home upset because they were bullied at school. Another child might be acting like a bully at school, reflecting tension or negative behavior learned at home. In some homes, siblings might engage in bullying each other, which can go unnoticed if parents see it as normal sibling rivalry. In this chapter, we will look at ways to handle bullying in the home environment, including dealing with siblings who bully, supporting a bullied child, and guiding a child who has been bullying others.

---

1. **Why Home Matters**
   Children spend many hours each day at home with siblings and parents or guardians. During these times, they see how adults settle conflicts and how siblings interact. If a child grows up in a calm, respectful atmosphere, they are more likely to develop those qualities themselves. If they see frequent shouting, name-calling, or physical aggression, they might assume this is how people are supposed to behave. Therefore, the home can either encourage bullying or help prevent it.

When families pay attention to bullying issues, they can step in early. They can notice if a child's mood changes or if they begin acting out. They can also talk openly about treating people with kindness, teaching children to use words instead of fists. This doesn't mean a household must be perfect—no home is—but parents who commit to fairness and respect set a positive example.

2. **Detecting Sibling Bullying**
   Sibling fights are common, but not all fights are bullying. In bullying, there is a power imbalance. One sibling might be significantly older, stronger, or more confident, and they regularly pick on the younger or more sensitive sibling. This can involve name-calling, threats, excluding them from family activities, or even physical harm. If the bullied sibling appears fearful, avoids the older sibling, or frequently complains of feeling hurt or humiliated, it might be bullying rather than a normal argument.

Parents sometimes overlook sibling bullying because they believe it is a normal part of growing up. However, if one child is consistently targeted and clearly distressed, parents should intervene. Telling them to "work it out on your own" might lead the younger or weaker sibling to feel helpless. Unchecked sibling bullying can also teach the bully that intimidation gets results, paving the way for bullying others at school.

Stopping Sibling Bullying
When parents see signs that one sibling is bullying another, they can take steps:

- **Lay Down Clear Rules**: Let children know that hurting or belittling each other is not allowed. This includes insults, threats, and physical aggression.
- **Supervise Interactions**: Keep an eye on how siblings talk to each other. If tension builds, step in before it escalates.
- **Promote Fairness**: Make sure chores, privileges, and responsibilities are balanced. Sometimes, jealousy or feeling slighted can spark bullying.
- **Teach Conflict Skills**: Show siblings how to talk about their disagreements calmly. If the older sibling is annoyed by the younger one, they should learn to say, "I need a little space right now," instead of pushing or calling names.
- **Use Consistent Consequences**: If bullying behavior continues, there should be fair but firm consequences, such as losing screen time or writing an apology letter. However, also consider teaching empathy by having them discuss how the bullied sibling feels.

These actions send the message that family members should protect and respect each other, not act like enemies in the same house.

Helping a Bullied Child at Home
When a child is bullied outside the home—whether at school or in the neighborhood—they often carry those feelings back home. Parents may notice changes in mood or behavior: the child might become quiet, anxious, or angry. They might have trouble sleeping or lose interest in activities they once enjoyed. A once-friendly child might snap at siblings more than usual. Recognizing these signs can help parents step in sooner.

Open communication is key. Asking questions such as "How was your day?" or "Did anything happen that made you feel upset?" can encourage the child to speak. If they admit to being bullied, parents can respond calmly, without anger or dismissiveness. Even though parents might feel upset, showing panic or intense anger might scare the child away from sharing more. It is often helpful to say, "I'm sorry this is happening to you. I believe you. Let's figure this out together."

Taking Action for a Bullied Child
If the bullying happens at school, parents can contact the teacher or counselor. They can describe what their child has said or any evidence they have—like text messages or pictures. Working with the school can lead to meetings where the bully is addressed, and steps are taken to protect the child. If the bullying occurs in the neighborhood, families might talk to community leaders, a local youth center, or the parents of the bully (if appropriate).

At home, parents can focus on building the child's self-confidence. They might help the child practice assertive responses, such as saying, "Leave me alone," or walking away to find an adult if they feel unsafe. Encouraging the child to maintain friendships and hobbies can also help them feel supported and remind them that not everyone treats them badly. Some children might benefit from therapy if the bullying has severely harmed their self-esteem or caused anxiety.

Handling a Child Who Bullies Others
It is difficult for many parents to accept that their child could be a bully. They might assume their child is just joking or that other kids are overly sensitive. However, if a teacher or other parent reports that a child is frequently picking on others, it is important to take it seriously. Brushing it off allows the behavior to grow. A child who bullies may do so for different reasons: they might be angry, seeking attention, or copying actions they observe at home.

First, parents can gather facts by talking to the school staff or community leaders who reported the bullying. What exactly happened? Was it a single incident or repeated behavior? Then, parents should speak calmly with the child, asking why they acted that way. It is important not to scream at them but to show seriousness. They should hear the child out while making it clear that hurting others is not acceptable.

Guiding a Bullying Child Toward Change
Once the issue is recognized, parents can take steps:

- **Set Non-Negotiable Rules**: Make it clear that hitting, threatening, or insulting others is never allowed.
- **Use Consequences That Teach**: If the child bullies, they might lose certain privileges, but also be required to do something constructive, like writing an apology or helping with tasks that build empathy.
- **Seek Underlying Causes**: Is the child stressed, unhappy, or dealing with something they cannot handle? A counselor can help uncover anger, sadness, or frustrations that lead to bullying.
- **Encourage Positive Outlets**: Direct the child's energy into sports, arts, or community service. This can teach teamwork and focus.
- **Model Respect**: Parents should treat each other, their children, and friends kindly. If a child sees parents using name-calling or threats, they might copy it.

This consistent approach can guide the bully to find healthier ways to express themselves and handle conflicts.

Managing Anger and Stress at Home
Some bullying arises when a child does not know how to deal with anger or stress. They might lash out at siblings or classmates. Teaching anger management at home can lower the risk of bullying. For example, parents can say, "When you feel your fists clench or your face get hot, that's a signal you're angry. Take a deep breath, step away, and let's talk about what's bothering you." By repeating this lesson, parents help the child form a new habit.

Families that face ongoing stress—like financial worries or a recent divorce—might find children becoming more irritable. If the child does not have a way to process these worries, they could turn to bullying as a release. In such cases, family counseling or talking to a trusted friend or relative can help the child cope better. It is important not to ignore changes in behavior but to address them with compassion.

Building Empathy at Home
Home is the best place to teach empathy. Parents can ask children how they think another person feels in a certain situation. If a sibling or friend is upset, they can guide the child to consider ways to help. Watching movies or reading stories that show characters facing struggles can spark conversations. "How do you think they felt when that happened? What would make them feel better?" By practicing these discussions, children learn to see beyond their own feelings.

Family volunteering is another way. Activities that involve helping neighbors or donating items to those in need can open children's eyes to different life experiences. While doing these actions, parents can talk about why helping is important. These lessons discourage bullying because children who develop empathy are less likely to enjoy harming or ridiculing others.

Encouraging Open Communication
Children who feel safe talking with their parents about anything—good or bad—are more likely to speak up if they are bullied or if they see bullying happening. Parents can build open communication by truly listening. That means setting aside phones, turning off the TV, and making eye contact when a child wants to share something. Even if parents are busy, they can say, "Let me finish this task, and then I want to hear more about that."

If a child confesses they made a mistake—like bullying or failing to help a classmate—parents should remain calm. They can thank the child for telling the truth and then discuss better choices. Reacting with rage or shame might push the child to hide the truth next time. By keeping trust alive, parents can continue guiding the child's moral development.

Establishing Family Rules About Technology
Cyberbullying often starts at home, where children use phones or computers. Parents can set rules on screen time, monitoring, and respectful online behavior. For example, no one in the family should post mean messages, gossip, or private pictures without permission. Parents might place computers in a shared area so they can see how children use social media. They can also encourage the child to talk to them if they receive nasty messages or see unkind posts.

When these rules are broken, parents should follow through with consequences—such as removing a phone for a set period. But again, they should also discuss why the rule is there. Stressing that online words can hurt just like spoken ones can help children understand the real impact of digital behavior. If a child is the target of cyberbullying, parents can document the harassment, block the bully, report it to the platform, and contact the school if classmates are involved.

Self-Esteem and Support at Home
Building a child's self-esteem can protect them from being either a target or a bully. When a child values themselves, they are less likely to feel the need to

push others down. They are also more likely to speak up if they are bullied, knowing they deserve respect. Parents can give specific praise, acknowledging a child's effort rather than focusing only on results. For example, "I'm proud of how much time you spent practicing piano," instead of just praising a perfect performance.

Quality family time helps too. Eating meals together, playing games, or talking about each other's day builds warmth and belonging. Children who feel connected at home have a strong base of support. They know they have people who care about their well-being, making them more resilient against bullying and less eager to harm others for attention or power.

Problem-Solving as a Family
When tension arises—maybe the child is angry about a teacher's decision or an issue with a friend—parents can use it as a chance to teach problem-solving. Instead of telling the child what to do, they can ask, "What are some ways we could handle this?" Then, they discuss each idea's pros and cons. This shows the child that challenges can be tackled with reasoning, not with shouting or threats. Over time, these skills help the child deal with peer conflicts calmly, lowering the urge to bully.

If siblings argue over who sits where in the car or who controls the game console, parents can guide them to find a compromise. For instance, maybe they take turns daily. Teaching these negotiation skills at home reduces the chance that a child will handle disagreements at school by pushing or insulting others. It also strengthens sibling relationships, making the home more peaceful.

Seeking Outside Help
Sometimes, family stress or a child's bullying actions run deeper than parents can manage alone. If parents notice that discipline and calm talks do not stop their child from bullying, or if a bullied child becomes depressed or anxious, professional help might be needed. Therapists or counselors can explore underlying problems, like anger issues, low self-esteem, or unresolved trauma.

Family therapy can also help if parents struggle to communicate with each other or with the child. It creates a space where everyone can express concerns with a trained expert guiding the discussion. This can be especially important if the child's bullying is tied to events at home—like divorce, a parent's illness, or conflict between family members.

Avoiding Mixed Messages

Children can be confused if parents say, "Don't bully," but then use hurtful language themselves. For example, calling the child names when angry or mocking neighbors behind their back. This teaches children that cruelty is acceptable if you are upset. To avoid mixed messages, parents should practice the respect they want their children to learn. That does not mean never feeling angry—it means showing that even when angry, you do not insult or threaten.

Additionally, parents can check the entertainment children consume. If a child watches shows or plays games that glorify picking on weaker characters, they might think that's funny. While banning all shows or games is not always the answer, parents can talk about the difference between fictional scenarios and real-life emotions. Encouraging children to think about how a character might feel can maintain empathy.

Helping Children Be Active Bystanders

Sometimes, the child at home might not be bullied or a bully, but they could see bullying happen. Parents can teach them how to be a helpful bystander. For example, they can encourage their child to stand next to the target and say, "That's not okay," or to get an adult. They can also remind them to avoid laughing or joining in if the group teases someone. Knowing they have family support to do the right thing can give children the courage to act. Later, parents can praise them for speaking up, reinforcing that it was a good deed.

Supporting Different Personality Types

Every child is unique. Some are shy and might be easily overwhelmed by teasing, while others are more outspoken. Parents can tailor their approach. If a child is very sensitive, teaching them gentle ways to set boundaries, like saying "Please stop," or seeking help can be important. If a child is naturally assertive, channeling that assertiveness into leadership and defending others can prevent them from turning to bullying.

In sibling dynamics, one child might be older and physically bigger. Reminding them that with power comes responsibility can help them see that bullying a younger sibling is unfair. On the other hand, the younger sibling might learn to speak up for themselves, with parents supporting them to do so calmly.

Maintaining Boundaries

Setting boundaries at home involves more than just telling children "no." It includes explaining why a rule exists. For example, if a parent says, "We do not hit in this family because hitting hurts people and we respect each other," they connect the rule to a value. This approach is often more effective than a simple demand. When children understand the reason behind a rule, they are more likely to follow it.

If a child breaks a boundary—like insulting a sibling—parents can calmly enforce consequences. The child might have to apologize or lose a privilege. By being consistent, parents show that these rules matter every day, not just when they feel like it. Over time, children internalize these limits, learning self-control and respect.

Handling Extended Family Dynamics
Sometimes, bullying behaviors can be learned from extended family members—like an older cousin who teases or a grandparent who uses harsh language. Parents can have polite talks with relatives, clarifying that they expect respectful treatment of their children. If the relatives ignore this, parents might limit visits or supervise them more closely. This can be tough, but children benefit from consistent messages about kindness and boundaries.

Additionally, children might see adult relatives argue or speak rudely. In these moments, parents can quietly explain to the child that the behavior is not ideal, reinforcing the family's own rules. It can be helpful for the child to see that even if some relatives behave poorly, the immediate family aims for more respectful communication.

Looking Toward a Peaceful Home
Addressing bullying at home is not just about ending negative behavior—it is about building a supportive environment where children feel valued and learn to value others. By spotting sibling bullying, guiding children who bully, and supporting those who are bullied, parents can prevent harmful cycles. With open talks, empathy lessons, and consistent boundaries, children learn skills that keep them from dragging conflict into bullying.

A peaceful home does not mean there are never arguments or that children never feel upset. It means disagreements do not spiral into insults or physical fights. It means each child knows they can speak up if they feel mistreated. It also means parents and children can work together to fix problems instead of letting them fester.

In the broader sense, a family that stands firmly against bullying often influences the community, too. Children who see respect in their homes carry that mindset to school, youth clubs, and friendships. By raising thoughtful, kind-hearted kids, parents send out ripples of positivity. Though bullying might appear in many forms, a strong, caring home is one of the best defenses. The lessons learned behind the front door can shape how children treat everyone they meet.

As we go forward, keep in mind that the family alone cannot solve every bullying problem. The child still interacts with classmates, neighbors, or online communities. Yet, the home is a primary source of comfort, guidance, and moral development. By facing bullying issues head-on—whether siblings, a child's own harmful actions, or the child being targeted—families become a safe haven where children gain the strength and wisdom to handle challenges in kinder ways.

Chapter 17: Restorative Strategies

When bullying happens, it is common to focus on discipline and punishment for the person who caused harm. While consequences can be useful, they do not always address the deeper reasons behind the behavior or help mend the hurt between the bully and the target. This is where restorative strategies can make a big difference. Restorative strategies look for ways to repair the damage done by bullying and encourage everyone involved to learn and grow. In this chapter, we will explore what restorative strategies are, how they help targets and those who bully, and why they can be an effective way to reduce bullying over time.

Understanding Restorative Strategies
Restorative strategies focus on healing relationships rather than just handing down punishments. The idea is that when bullying happens, harm is done not only to the target but also to the overall community. People may feel unsafe, angry, or disappointed. Restorative approaches ask everyone involved—including the target, the person who bullied, and sometimes witnesses or bystanders—to take part in finding a solution. This might involve talking about what happened, sharing how each person feels, and coming up with ways to fix the harm.

Instead of separating the bully from the group through suspension or isolation, restorative strategies bring them together with the target in a safe, guided setting. This does not mean the bully gets away without facing any consequences. Rather, it means the bully must own up to their actions, hear about the pain they caused, and find a way to make things right. If done well, this approach can reduce the chance of bullying happening again. It also aims to show the bully how to treat people better in the future.

Why Restorative Strategies Matter
When we rely only on punishment, the child who bullies may feel angry, ashamed, or misunderstood. They might lash out again, believing no one cares to understand why they acted that way. Meanwhile, the target may not get the chance to express how the bullying hurt them, which can leave them feeling unheard or unsafe. Restorative strategies tackle both issues. They teach the person who bullied about empathy and responsibility, and they give the target a voice in what should happen next.

Key Principles of Restorative Approaches

- **Focus on Harm**: The goal is to address the harm caused and ways to fix it, rather than just dishing out penalties.
- **Responsibility**: The person who caused harm must admit their actions and commit to changing.
- **Inclusion**: Everyone affected has a role in deciding the outcome. This might include parents, teachers, or friends who witnessed the bullying.
- **Healing Relationships**: The plan should help repair trust between the bully and the target, if it is possible and safe.
- **Future Safety**: The process aims to make sure the target feels protected moving forward.

Examples of Restorative Practices

- **Restorative Circles**: A group sits in a circle with a trained facilitator. The facilitator asks questions like "What happened?" "Who was hurt?" and "How can we fix this?" Each person has a chance to speak without being interrupted. The circle might involve the target, the person who bullied, classmates who saw the incident, and sometimes parents or counselors.
- **Mediation Sessions**: This involves a neutral mediator who meets with the target and the person who bullied. The mediator helps them communicate feelings and come up with a plan to prevent future harm.
- **Letters of Apology**: The person who bullied might write a letter explaining how they realize their behavior was wrong, showing that they understand the impact. This is not just a quick "I'm sorry," but a deeper reflection.
- **Repair Activities**: If the bullying involved property damage or destruction, the bully might fix or replace what they broke. Or if the bullying was verbal, they might do community service or help in some project chosen by the target.

How Restorative Circles Work

A restorative circle usually includes a few important steps:

- **Preparation**: A teacher, counselor, or facilitator talks separately with the target and the bully to explain how the process works. They make sure everyone feels safe and ready to speak openly. The facilitator also sets

ground rules, such as no name-calling and letting each person finish speaking.
- **Sharing**: During the circle, everyone sits in a way that allows eye contact. One by one, each person explains what happened from their point of view. This might include how they felt during the bullying and how they feel now.
- **Feelings and Impact**: The circle then explores how the bullying affected the target's emotions, the bully's emotions, and even how bystanders felt watching it all. This stage can be powerful, because it forces the person who bullied to see the real pain caused by their words or actions.
- **Finding Solutions**: The group discusses what can be done to repair the harm. This could include an apology, returning or paying for damaged items, or agreeing on new ways to behave. It might also involve the bully participating in kindness exercises or reflection tasks.
- **Agreement**: Everyone in the circle agrees to the plan. They might sign a simple contract stating what each person will do. This agreement sets clear expectations so that the problem does not just fade away without real change.

Benefits for the Target

Targets often feel powerless during bullying. Restorative strategies let them have a voice in deciding how things will be resolved. They can say, "This is what I need to feel safe again," or "This is how you can make up for what you did." Having that control can help them heal. It can also give them closure, especially if they get a genuine apology. Many targets find it meaningful to see the bully realize how hurtful their actions were.

Benefits for the Person Who Bullied

Children or teens who bully might not understand the depth of harm they cause. A quick punishment like suspension may not change their mindset. But in a restorative approach, they must listen to the target's feelings. This can spark empathy, making them less likely to bully again. Also, they get a chance to repair the relationship. Instead of being labeled a "bad kid," they can show that they want to learn from their mistakes. This can improve their self-worth in a healthier way, rather than feeling they must keep bullying to appear powerful.

Challenges and Safeguards

Not every situation is right for a restorative approach. If the target feels too scared to face the bully, forcing a meeting can make things worse. In severe cases, or when there is a real danger, a school might need to use stronger protective measures first. The target's comfort is key—if they do not want to participate in a restorative meeting, that choice should be respected. Also, the person who bullied must be willing to try this path and show real remorse, rather than faking it to avoid punishment.

A trained facilitator can help ensure that the process is fair and not just another way for the bully to intimidate the target. This might mean having separate sessions at first, to build trust before bringing the two sides together. Some schools have staff specifically trained in these practices, while others bring in outside experts.

Restorative Practices in Schools
Many schools now include restorative strategies in their anti-bullying policies. Instead of automatically suspending a bully, administrators might check if the situation can be handled with a restorative meeting. If both parties agree, and the bullying is not extreme, the school arranges a session. If the process goes well, the bully may avoid harsher penalties, but they must follow the agreement that comes out of the session. If they break that agreement, the school can use regular disciplinary steps.

Schools might also use restorative practices in everyday life, not just for bullying. For example, if two students argue in class, the teacher can organize a quick circle to talk it out. By making these conversations normal, students get used to facing conflicts openly rather than letting them fester. Over time, this can improve the school's overall climate.

Using Restorative Strategies at Home
Families can try simpler forms of restorative approaches at home. If siblings argue or one sibling bullies the other, parents can bring them together calmly. Each sibling gets a chance to say how they felt. Then, they discuss ways to fix the hurt. This might mean an apology, a plan to share chores more fairly, or a commitment to stop using mean words. Parents act like facilitators, ensuring each child has a turn and no one interrupts with yelling or blaming. This can teach siblings that conflict can be resolved in a constructive way.

Building Empathy Through Storytelling
Sometimes, restorative work involves hearing stories from both sides. The bully might explain that they felt lonely or under pressure from peers, so they lashed

out. The target might describe how they lost confidence and cried at night. Hearing these stories can change how each side sees the other. Instead of a vague sense of anger, they understand the human feelings behind the actions. This empathy does not excuse the bullying, but it helps everyone see that real people were hurt and that the solution requires compassion as well as accountability.

Questions Asked in Restorative Sessions
Facilitators often use open-ended questions that allow people to express themselves clearly. For example:

- **To the Person Who Bullied**: "What made you decide to act this way?" "Who do you think was harmed by your actions?" "How can you fix what you've done?"
- **To the Target**: "How did this affect you?" "What do you need to feel safe again?" "How can the group support you?"
- **To Bystanders**: "What was it like watching this happen?" "How did it affect you or your sense of safety?" "What can we do as a group to keep it from happening again?"

Healing the Group
Bullying does not just harm the target. It can make bystanders nervous or guilty for not helping. It can damage the overall trust in a classroom or a team. Restorative circles allow those bystanders to express how uncomfortable they felt or how they regret not stepping in. When they share these feelings, they might realize that they have a role in preventing future bullying. The group can decide on new norms, like agreeing to speak up if they see bullying. This way, the problem is not just between the bully and the target—it becomes a community concern with a shared solution.

Long-Term Changes
When done well, restorative strategies can reduce the likelihood of the bully repeating their actions. They learn that their behavior has real consequences, not just in terms of punishments, but in how it impacts other people's feelings. They also build skills for handling conflict without aggression. Meanwhile, the target gains closure and a sense that the harm has been recognized and addressed, which can speed healing.

Over the long term, schools that use restorative approaches often see fewer repeat offenses and a safer environment. Students become familiar with the idea that if they harm someone, they will have to face that person's feelings directly. They cannot just brush it aside or hide behind a simple detention. By focusing on relationships, the school encourages empathy and accountability.

When Restorative Approaches Might Not Work
Not all bullying situations are suitable for restorative strategies. Some forms of bullying are extreme, involving serious threats or violence, and they might require immediate protective actions. Also, if a bully shows no remorse or if the target is too frightened, pushing them together could do more harm. In certain cases—like repeated bullying over a long period—there might be a need for separate interventions first, ensuring the target's safety. A skilled counselor or facilitator can help decide if a restorative meeting is appropriate and safe for everyone involved.

Training and Support
For restorative strategies to work, facilitators need proper training. They must know how to keep the conversation balanced and respectful, preventing it from turning into more blame. Schools and communities often have training programs for teachers, administrators, and even older students who want to serve as peer mediators. Support from school leaders is crucial. If principals, counselors, and teachers all believe in this approach, it is more likely to be successful. Sometimes, these sessions can be time-consuming, but the payoff is a healthier school climate.

Combining Restorative Practices with Other Measures
Restorative strategies should not replace all other steps. They work best alongside clear anti-bullying policies, consistent discipline for severe cases, and lessons on empathy and communication. For instance, a student might complete a restorative session and also attend counseling sessions on managing anger or stress. Another might sign an agreement not to contact the target online, combined with losing certain privileges if they break that agreement. When used together, these measures create a comprehensive approach to preventing and dealing with bullying.

Encouraging a Caring Community
At their core, restorative methods encourage kindness and mutual responsibility. They show students and adults that the goal is not just to punish wrongdoing,

but to fix harm and rebuild trust. Over time, this can shift how people view conflict. Instead of hiding or denying problems, they learn to tackle them openly, focusing on the feelings and needs of everyone involved. This sense of caring can spread beyond the walls of a single classroom, influencing how students treat each other in hallways, online, and outside of school.

Voices of Experience

Students who have gone through restorative circles sometimes say they were nervous at first but felt relief afterward. Targets often report feeling validated—that their pain was seen and taken seriously. Bullies may say they finally understood the emotional damage they caused. Some even form better relationships after the process, moving past anger and fear. While these outcomes are not guaranteed in every case, they show the potential for true change when people face each other honestly.

Parents also play a role. They might join these sessions to support their child and hear how the behavior affected others. Seeing the target's hurt can be a wake-up call, leading them to address problems at home or seek therapy for their child. Likewise, a target's parents might feel reassured to know that the issue is not being brushed under the rug and that the bully is being held accountable in a meaningful way.

Looking Ahead

Restorative strategies will not magically erase bullying. Yet they offer a path that invites understanding, responsibility, and healing. By focusing on repairing harm instead of just handing out punishments, these methods can reach the human side of every conflict. Bullies learn that causing pain has real costs. Targets find a safe space to share their hurt and ask for what they need. The community sees that everyone is responsible for keeping each other safe. As more schools and families adopt restorative approaches, bullying can become less frequent, and when it does happen, there is a better chance for true resolution. Through empathy, communication, and a focus on solutions, restorative strategies support a culture of respect—one in which everyone's dignity is valued and protected.

Chapter 18: Empowering Bystanders

When bullying takes place, we usually focus on the bully and the target. But there is another group that plays an important role: the bystanders. Bystanders are people who see or hear the bullying but are not directly involved as the main person doing the bullying or being harmed. They might be classmates, friends, teammates, or just kids walking by when an incident happens. Bystanders can either remain silent, making the bully feel more powerful, or they can step up to help, reducing the harm and possibly stopping the bullying. In this chapter, we will talk about why bystanders are so important, how they can safely intervene, and how schools and families can support them in taking a stand against bullying.

---

1. **Why Bystanders Matter**
   Bystanders form the audience of bullying. If a bully sees that people are laughing, watching with amusement, or not saying anything, they may feel encouraged. They think their behavior is approved or at least not challenged. On the other hand, when bystanders speak up—telling the bully to stop, or helping the target get away—the bully loses social power. Bystanders can change the situation quickly by showing that bullying is not accepted. In many cases, the presence of even one confident bystander is enough to make a bully back down.
2. **Types of Bystanders**
   Not all bystanders act the same way. Here are a few common types:
- **Silent Observers**: They watch what is happening but say nothing. They might worry about becoming a new target if they interfere.
- **Encouragers**: Some bystanders laugh, cheer, or tease along with the bully, even if they do not start the bullying themselves.
- **Helpers**: These bystanders step in to defend the target, speak out against the bully, or get an adult's help. They might also comfort the target afterward.

One reason bystanders stay silent is fear. They might be scared the bully will turn on them, or they might not know what to do. Another reason is peer pressure—if the bully or their friends are popular, challenging them can feel risky. Yet bystanders have more power than they realize. Even small acts of kindness can help a target feel less alone.

Why It Is Hard for Bystanders to Intervene
Many children say they would like to help if they saw someone being bullied, but in the moment, they freeze. They might wonder, "Will this make me the next target?" or "Will my friends think I am weird for defending someone unpopular?" They might also think, "Maybe I am misunderstanding the situation," or "It's none of my business." This hesitation can be strong, especially if the child has never been taught how to intervene. Teaching bystanders to act safely and confidently can ease these fears.

Ways Bystanders Can Help
Bystanders can step up in different ways. Each situation might call for a different response:

- **Direct Action**: Telling the bully in a firm voice to stop, or stepping between the bully and the target if it is safe to do so.
- **Distracting**: Creating a diversion that interrupts the bullying, such as asking the target a random question ("Hey, can I borrow a pencil?") so they can walk away.
- **Offering Comfort**: Checking on the target afterward, inviting them to leave the area, or saying, "That was wrong, are you okay?" This gives support to the target and shows they are not alone.
- **Reporting**: If a bystander feels unsafe confronting the bully, they can tell a teacher, coach, counselor, or another trusted adult. In online cases, they might report the post or message to the platform.
- **Gathering Friends**: A bystander might not want to act alone. Asking a group of friends to stand together against the bully can be more effective and less risky.

Standing Up vs. Staying Safe
Bystanders should not be expected to put themselves in danger. Sometimes, the bully is much bigger or shows signs of being violent. In those cases, going directly against the bully might cause harm to the bystander. That does not mean they must do nothing. They can still help by quickly finding an adult or calling for help. They might also record details in a safe way (like remembering the place, date, and names) to share later. The goal is for bystanders to intervene in ways that are effective without putting themselves at serious risk.

Teaching Children to Be Helpers

Schools and families can teach children that everyone shares the responsibility of creating a safe environment. This includes showing how to be a helper when bullying occurs. For example:

- **Role-Playing**: In class or at home, children can practice scenarios. One plays the bully, another the target, and a third is the bystander. They learn phrases like, "This isn't right. Let's go find a teacher," or "We don't treat people like that here."
- **Discussing Real Situations**: If bullying happens in the community, adults can talk about what bystanders did or did not do, and how things might have turned out differently with a certain intervention.
- **Highlighting Acts of Bravery**: When a child does speak up, praise that behavior. Let them know it was the right thing to do.
- **Teaching Group Support**: Encourage children to stand with at least one other friend when they see bullying. Acting in pairs or groups is safer and more convincing.

The Role of Schools in Empowering Bystanders

Schools can create a culture where helping is the norm. They might develop "buddy programs" pairing older students with younger ones or set up peer support teams that watch out for students who seem isolated. Teachers can remind students daily that if they see bullying, they should tell someone. Posters around the school can say, "Speak up. We have your back." Some schools have anonymous tip lines where students can text or drop a note, allowing them to report bullying without fear. When the school responds positively, students learn that speaking up makes a difference.

Helping Bystanders Overcome Fear

Fear is the biggest barrier. One way to reduce it is by having open discussions about what happens when people do speak up. Often, bullies back off if they realize they are outnumbered or if an adult is coming. Children can also be reminded that if they see the bully after they have intervened, they can stay near friends or safe areas. Over time, stories of successful bystander interventions can reassure children that they are not alone.

What If the Bystander Is a Friend of the Bully?

Sometimes the bystander is close to the bully. They may worry that speaking up will cost them that friendship. In these cases, it can help to remind them that true friends do not force you to do wrong things. If the bully is a real friend, they may listen when the bystander says, "Don't do that." If they refuse and punish the bystander for standing up, that signals the relationship might not be a healthy one. Schools can also encourage respectful friend groups. When children see that popularity does not excuse cruelty, they might be more willing to challenge a friend's bullying behavior.

Recognizing Subtle Bullying
Bystanders might not realize they are seeing bullying if it is not physical. Verbal bullying (like cruel jokes, name-calling) or social bullying (like spreading rumors or excluding someone) can be overlooked. Teaching children to notice patterns—someone consistently making fun of another or ignoring them from group tasks—can help them recognize that it is not just harmless teasing. When they see it, they can offer a kind word to the target or let an adult know.

Online Bystanders
Cyberbullying has its own set of bystanders. They might see mean comments, embarrassing photos, or hateful messages in group chats or social media. Some might even "like" or share the post, not thinking about the pain it causes. Others silently watch, not knowing how to help. Online bystanders can intervene by posting positive comments to counteract the negativity, reporting harmful content to the platform, or sending the target a supportive private message. They can also avoid forwarding any hurtful material. Just like in-person bullying, a single online voice can shift the tone of the conversation.

Encouraging Empathy in Bystanders
One way to empower bystanders is by strengthening their empathy. If children imagine what it feels like to be the target—embarrassed, anxious, lonely—they are more likely to act. Schools might share stories or short films showing how bullying damages people's emotions, helping children see that silence allows cruelty to grow. Some teachers assign writing exercises like, "If you saw someone being hurt, what would you do?" or "Write about a time you felt alone and needed help." These assignments prompt reflection, making children more aware of the needs of others.

Bystander Intervention Skills
It helps to teach practical skills rather than just telling kids, "Help if you see bullying." For example:

- **Using the Child's Name**: "Hey, Jordan, come with me for a second," can pull the target away from a bully.
- **Polite but Firm Statements**: "That's not okay," or "Leave them alone," said in a confident tone, can disrupt the bullying.
- **Getting Help Quickly**: Knowing which adult to approach and what to say, such as "There's a problem in the hallway," can prevent more harm.
- **Social Support**: Teaming up with a friend to approach the target, "Hey, do you want to hang out with us?" can help the target escape the situation.

Handling Backlash

Sometimes, a bully might react angrily toward a bystander who steps in. Schools and parents can prepare children for this possibility by discussing safety plans and ensuring that staff will protect them if retaliation occurs. If a child is harassed for defending someone, the school should treat it as a serious offense. This shows the entire student body that standing against bullying is backed by the adults in charge. When bystanders see that they will be supported, they are less likely to be silent.

Building a Supportive Peer Culture

Children are more willing to be helpers if they sense that their peers approve of that behavior. Peer culture shifts when enough students begin to see kindness as a strength rather than a weakness. This can start with small groups of friends who pledge not to laugh at bullying or who decide to stand by each other if one of them speaks up. Over time, their example can influence others. Teachers and counselors might encourage these small efforts by praising them in class, making them visible role models for younger students.

Parent Involvement

Parents can also help children become effective bystanders. At home, they can talk about what to do if a friend bullies someone or if they see a stranger being mocked. Parents can share stories from their own lives or from news articles where bystanders made a difference. They can ask, "What would you do in that situation? How could you help?" Practicing or discussing these scenarios prepares children mentally. Parents can also reassure them that if they intervene safely, the parent will stand behind them and speak to the school if problems arise.

Small Acts That Make a Difference

Bystander intervention does not always have to be dramatic. Sometimes, a quiet word or a simple gesture helps a target feel supported. Even after the bullying stops, the bystander can walk over to the target and say, "That wasn't right. Are you okay?" They might invite the target to join their table at lunch or partner with them in a class activity. These small acts break the isolation bullying often creates. Targets who feel less alone are more likely to recover and speak up for themselves in the future.

Stories of Positive Bystander Action
Schools sometimes share real examples where students saved the day by standing up for someone. Hearing these stories can inspire others. For instance, a girl might have stepped in when a group of older boys teased a younger student on the bus. By calmly telling them to stop and pressing the bus driver's alert button, she ended the incident. Or in another case, a group of classmates might have confronted someone sharing hurtful rumors, saying, "Stop. That's not fair," until the rumor-spreader gave up. Celebrating these successes (without using the forbidden word or synonyms) encourages more children to do the same.

Shifting from Watching to Acting
Many children describe a moment of realization: "I saw them crying, and I knew I had to do something." This shift from passive watching to taking action can happen if they have been taught that it is their right and responsibility to help. Also, reminding them that a situation might look scary at first, but with friends or adults backing them up, they can make a big difference. Over time, the more children practice stepping in—even in small ways—the more natural it becomes.

Looking Ahead
Empowering bystanders is a key piece of the puzzle in fighting bullying. When children understand that their silence can be taken as approval, and when they learn that speaking up can stop bullying or at least support the target, a real shift happens. Schools and families can support bystanders by teaching safe, realistic strategies, by praising them for their bravery, and by ensuring that if they do speak up, they will not face retaliation alone. This shared responsibility changes the entire environment. Instead of letting bullying thrive, bystanders become allies for each other, showing that kindness is a community effort. Through their combined voice, they remind everyone that hurting others is never okay—and that help is always close by.

Chapter 19: Models and Practices That Help

Many people agree that bullying is a serious problem, but they sometimes struggle to find effective, lasting ways to stop it. That is where specific models and practices can help. These models give step-by-step frameworks for schools, families, and communities to reduce bullying behaviors and build safer environments. Each practice has its own ideas, but they all share a common goal: to keep children from harming one another and to help them grow into kinder, more responsible individuals. In this chapter, we will look at different models and practices that have been successful in various places. We will explore how they work and how they can be adapted to fit different groups or age levels.

Whole-School Approach
One of the most popular models for addressing bullying is the whole-school approach. The idea is simple: make sure that anti-bullying efforts do not happen in only one part of the school day (like during an assembly) or in just one classroom. Instead, the entire school works together—teachers, administrators, staff, students, and even families—to set a consistent tone against bullying.

- **Shared Vision**: From the principal to the cafeteria staff, everyone agrees that bullying is not allowed. They learn to recognize it, speak against it, and support targets.
- **Clear Policies**: The school has simple, well-known rules about bullying. Students know what to do if they see it, and staff know how to respond.
- **Staff Training**: Teachers, bus drivers, and other employees get regular training on spotting bullying behaviors and handling them quickly.
- **Student Involvement**: Students take part in creating anti-bullying posters, discussing guidelines, and leading peer support clubs. When students feel ownership, they are more likely to follow the rules.
- **Parent Partnerships**: The school sends newsletters or holds meetings to inform parents about bullying policies. Parents learn what signs to watch for at home and how to help their children.

A whole-school approach often includes routines like greeting students at the classroom door, holding short "check-in" meetings, and celebrating acts of kindness. Over time, these small moments set a positive atmosphere that fights bullying in a subtle but powerful way.

Social and Emotional Learning (SEL)
Social and Emotional Learning (SEL) is a model that focuses on teaching children important life skills such as empathy, self-control, responsible decision-making, and relationship-building. While SEL can address many issues, it is especially helpful in preventing bullying because it teaches children to understand their own emotions and the feelings of others.

- **Self-Awareness**: Children learn to notice when they feel angry, sad, or jealous. This awareness can keep them from lashing out at others.
- **Self-Management**: They practice calming strategies like deep breathing or counting to ten, helping them handle stress without hurting peers.
- **Social Awareness**: They learn to recognize how their words or actions can affect someone else. Lessons in empathy teach them to imagine themselves in another person's place.
- **Relationship Skills**: They work on cooperation, active listening, and conflict resolution, making it easier to get along without resorting to bullying.
- **Responsible Decision-Making**: Children learn to think before acting and to consider the consequences of hurting someone.

Schools that adopt SEL often integrate it into regular lessons, such as reading a story and discussing the characters' emotions, or practicing group work in ways that encourage sharing and kindness. Over time, students become more thoughtful about their actions.

Peer Mediation Programs
Peer mediation is a practice where selected students learn to help their classmates resolve conflicts. Typically, these trained students (known as "peer mediators") act as neutral helpers during an argument, guiding both sides to explain their viewpoints and discover a fair solution.

- **Selection of Peer Mediators**: Students who show good listening skills and fairness are chosen. They receive extra training on communication and problem-solving.
- **Mediation Sessions**: If two classmates are in conflict (which might include bullying), they can go to the peer mediators for help. The mediators set ground rules, listen to each side, and ask questions.

- **Finding Agreement**: After each person shares, the mediators help them brainstorm solutions. The goal is for both sides to feel heard and to come up with a plan to end the conflict.
- **Adult Oversight**: A counselor or teacher usually supervises to ensure the session stays respectful and safe.

Peer mediation can build trust among students. When classmates see that conflicts can be solved in a calm way, they are less likely to turn to mean behavior. Also, bullies might become more aware that their actions will not remain hidden if their peers openly oppose them.

Olweus Bullying Prevention Program

Created by psychologist Dan Olweus, this is one of the oldest and most studied anti-bullying programs in the world. It is designed for elementary, middle, and junior high schools. Key features include:

- **School Surveys**: First, students fill out surveys about bullying. This helps the school see what kind of problems are most common and where they happen (like hallways, playgrounds, or online).
- **Staff Training**: Teachers and other staff learn how to spot bullying, intervene on the spot, and follow up. They also learn ways to foster positive teacher-student relationships.
- **Classroom Rules**: Teachers lead weekly talks about bullying, empathy, and respect. They post clear rules like "We do not bully others" and "We try to help students who are bullied."
- **Parent Involvement**: Parents learn the school's rules so they can reinforce them at home. They might also receive tips on handling bullying if it occurs.
- **Consistent Consequences**: When bullying happens, staff respond in a predictable way—talking with the bully, informing parents, and creating a plan to prevent repeats.

Schools using this program often see drops in bullying incidents because everyone has a common language and approach.

KiVa Program

KiVa is a research-based program that started in Finland. It focuses on preventing bullying and stopping it quickly if it does occur. Unique points include:

- **Virtual Learning**: Students play online games and complete activities that teach them how to handle bullying. They practice recognizing it, standing up for targets, and showing kindness.
- **Class Lessons**: Teachers run lessons about empathy, group dynamics, and the role of bystanders. The lessons aim to shift the social environment so bullying is not admired.
- **Specialist Team**: A KiVa team at the school (usually teachers or counselors) investigates bullying cases. They talk to the bully, the target, and bystanders to create a plan.
- **Positive Peer Influence**: KiVa strongly encourages classmates to use their power for good by supporting each other instead of backing the bully.

Research has shown KiVa can greatly reduce bullying, especially if the school commits to it fully. Some schools see drops in peer victimization, and students report feeling safer.

Mentorship and Role Models

Another helpful practice is pairing children with mentors or role models who show empathy and respect. This can be done in various ways:

- **Older Students as Mentors**: High school students might visit younger grades to discuss bullying and lead small group talks. Younger children often look up to older kids, so hearing them say, "Kindness counts," can have a big impact.
- **Community Mentors**: Trusted adults, such as local leaders, coaches, or volunteers, can spend time with children who are at risk of bullying or being bullied. These adults listen, guide, and encourage positive behaviors.
- **Teacher Mentorship**: A teacher might adopt a more personal mentoring role for a student who struggles socially. They check in daily, help the student set goals, and coach them on handling conflicts.

Seeing a caring adult handle stress or disagreements calmly teaches children better ways to act. Mentorship shows them they are valued, which can reduce the desire to bully or allow bullying.

Positive Behavior Interventions and Supports (PBIS)

PBIS is a broad approach for improving overall behavior in schools, including bullying prevention. It focuses on teaching and rewarding the behavior schools want to see:

- **Behavior Expectations**: The school picks a few simple rules like "Be Respectful," "Be Responsible," and "Be Safe." These are displayed everywhere.
- **Direct Teaching**: Teachers show what each rule looks like in the classroom, hallway, cafeteria, etc. For example, "Being Respectful" in the hallway might mean walking quietly and not teasing others.
- **Recognition**: Staff members praise or reward students who follow the rules or show kindness. This could be a note, a sticker, or a small acknowledgment. Over time, students see that good behavior gets positive attention.
- **Data Tracking**: Schools track behavior incidents to see patterns and respond quickly. If bullying spikes in a certain hallway, staff increase monitoring there.

PBIS does not replace other anti-bullying efforts, but it adds a layer of positivity. By setting clear, positive rules, the approach can lower aggression and encourage empathy.

Safe Spaces and Trusted Adults

Sometimes, bullying happens in hidden corners or online, leaving targets feeling alone. A key practice is creating safe spaces and linking children to trusted adults:

- **Designated Zones**: Certain spots in the school—like the counselor's office or a specially supervised area—can be known as safe zones where a child can go if they feel threatened.
- **Open-Door Policy**: Teachers and staff can let students know they are always ready to listen. This might mean having a visible sign that says, "If you need help, please knock."
- **Advisory Periods**: Some schools set aside a short time each day or week for students to check in with a teacher they trust. If bullying occurs, the child can talk about it in this relaxed setting.

When children know there is a place or person they can run to, they are less likely to hide the bullying. They feel supported, and bullies have fewer opportunities to act in secret.

Multi-Tiered Support Systems
Some children need more help than others. A multi-tiered system arranges support in levels:

- **Tier 1**: Everyone gets basic lessons on kindness, conflict resolution, and bullying prevention.
- **Tier 2**: Children at risk of bullying or being bullied get small group sessions on social skills or anger management.
- **Tier 3**: Children who repeatedly bully or are severely affected by bullying receive one-on-one counseling or specialized programs.

By matching the intensity of support to each child's needs, schools can use resources effectively. Those who just need a reminder about kindness get it at Tier 1, while those who need deeper help get it at Tier 3.

Encouraging Family-School Collaboration
Effective models do not stop at the school doors. They link with families so that messages about respect and empathy continue at home. This can happen through:

- **Parent Workshops**: Schools might hold sessions where parents learn about bullying signs, how to talk to children about kindness, and the school's anti-bullying plan.
- **Shared Language**: If the school says "We solve problems with words, not fists," parents can repeat the same phrase at home.
- **Home-School Journals**: Younger students might bring home a short diary for parents to sign, showing daily or weekly efforts to behave kindly.

When the school and parents send the same message, children are less confused about what is right and wrong. This unity makes anti-bullying lessons stronger.

Repeated Education and Reinforcement
Models that work well usually stress that you cannot teach kindness once and be done. Children need reminders:

- **Regular Lessons**: Short lessons or discussions on treating others well should happen often, not just during special "Bullying Awareness Week."
- **Reflection Activities**: At the end of the day or week, students can reflect on how they handled conflicts or helped a peer.

- **Check-Ins**: Teachers might ask: "Did anyone see a classmate do something kind this week?" Hearing real examples from classmates can inspire others.

Constant reinforcement helps keep the topic fresh. If it becomes routine, kindness and respect become part of everyday life instead of a one-time lesson.

Leadership from School Officials
Leaders like principals or superintendents have a big influence on whether models and practices actually work. If they talk about bullying prevention in staff meetings, budget for training, and praise teachers who manage conflicts well, the whole staff sees it as important. If a principal ignores reports of bullying or fails to provide resources, even the best program can fade. Leadership sets the tone and shows that the school is serious about making changes.

Adapting Models to Different Ages
A model that works for high schoolers might need some changes for elementary kids. Younger children may respond better to simple stories, coloring activities, or puppet shows, while teens might want group discussions, role-plays, or peer-led workshops. The key is to keep the core principles—empathy, respect, and accountability—while presenting them in age-friendly ways. For instance, a high school might hold regular group talks about online bullying and personal boundaries, while a kindergarten class might role-play how to ask nicely for a toy.

Emphasizing Positive Peer Influence
Many models now focus on bystanders (or witnesses) because they are often the largest group. Teaching children that they have a duty to step in, or at least report bullying, can flip the power dynamic. Programs like KiVa and Olweus place strong emphasis on making sure bystanders do not stay silent. This can include lessons where students practice phrases like "Leave them alone," or "That's not okay," so they feel ready if they see bullying. Over time, the bully realizes that the group does not support them, which can reduce their behavior.

Gathering Data and Measuring Success
Programs that keep good records can adjust their methods over time. They might:

- **Survey Students**: Ask how often they see bullying, where it happens, and how safe they feel at school.

- **Track Incidents**: Note how many bullying reports come in each month, in which locations, and at what times.
- **Review Outcomes**: If a certain grade level has more problems, the school might add extra lessons for that group. If physical bullying is down but cyberbullying is up, they might add digital safety workshops.

Being able to see trends helps schools fine-tune their approach. It also shows if a certain program is working—if rates of bullying drop after six months, that is a good sign. If not, the school may try a different approach or improve training.

Addressing Specific Challenges
Some forms of bullying call for extra steps. For example:

- **Cyberbullying**: Schools might add lessons on responsible online behavior, how to block or report abusive users, and how to avoid spreading hurtful content.
- **Bias-Based Bullying**: If children are teased because of their race, religion, or disability, programs need to teach respect for differences. Cultural awareness sessions or celebrating each child's background can help reduce prejudice.
- **Bullying Involving Physical Harm**: If there is violence, the school might coordinate with local law enforcement or mental health services, ensuring everyone stays safe while the bully receives help.

Adapting models to these challenges is vital for truly effective solutions.

Community-Wide Involvement
Sometimes, bullying spills over into community centers, sports leagues, or online platforms outside of school. A full approach might invite coaches, youth leaders, and local business owners to learn about the school's anti-bullying policies. They can share consistent messages like "We treat each other with respect, no matter where we are." Libraries or community centers might post guidelines on kindness, reminding everyone that bullying is not accepted. When children see the same messages everywhere, they realize respect is a community value, not just a school rule.

Mentoring Younger Children
In many models, older students volunteer to lead anti-bullying talks or activities for younger children. By hearing from older peers, younger kids often pay more attention. Meanwhile, older students gain leadership experience and practice

empathy. Some schools even create "buddy benches" on playgrounds. If a child feels lonely or is being teased, they sit on the bench, and older volunteers or classmates go over and invite them to join a game.

Continuous Improvement
Each year brings new students, staff changes, and evolving social media platforms. That is why no model can remain unchanged forever. Effective programs often have committees or teams that meet regularly to assess what is working. They might find that after one year, physical bullying is down, but name-calling is still high. Then they adjust lessons to stress respectful language. This ongoing process ensures that the school stays ahead of new bullying trends.

Looking Forward
Models and practices are not quick fixes—they are guides for consistent action. Whether it is a whole-school approach, an SEL curriculum, peer mediation, or a structured program like Olweus or KiVa, the aim is the same: to help children treat each other with kindness and respect. Each model may require time, training, and teamwork. But when schools, families, and communities commit to these approaches, they create safer spaces where bullying struggles to thrive.

Over time, these efforts can become part of a school's or community's identity. Children grow up knowing that meanness will not be tolerated. They learn healthy ways to handle anger, frustration, and peer pressure. In short, these models and practices do more than just stop negative behaviors—they help children build stronger, happier connections with others. By focusing on empathy, responsibility, and understanding, we give each child the chance to learn and grow without fear. This is how real change takes hold, making sure that bullying becomes less common and that support, respect, and care become the everyday norm.

Chapter 20: Supporting Positive Relationships

Bullying often begins where relationships have broken down or never started well. A child who feels alone might lash out. A child who wants to impress peers might show off by teasing someone else. A group that excludes a new student can turn that exclusion into bullying. On the flip side, when children have strong, caring connections with family, friends, and community members, they are less likely to bully or be bullied. This final chapter looks at how we can support positive relationships in all parts of a child's life—at home, at school, and beyond—and how these relationships serve as a shield against bullying.

Why Positive Relationships Matter
Strong relationships build trust, understanding, and a sense of belonging. Children who feel close to others learn to handle conflicts more calmly because they do not want to hurt someone they care about. They also have people to turn to if they are targeted by bullying. Over time, feeling supported helps them develop self-worth, making it less likely they will pick on someone else for a feeling of power.

Creating Emotional Safety at Home
The home is often the first place children learn about relationships. Parents, guardians, and siblings can encourage emotional safety by:

- **Listening Actively**: Put aside distractions when a child talks, maintaining eye contact and nodding to show understanding. This tells them their words matter.
- **Showing Empathy**: If a child is upset, recognize their feelings, saying something like, "I see you're feeling sad. Can you tell me more about why?"
- **Consistent Rules**: Having fair and predictable rules at home helps children feel secure. They know what to expect if they break a rule, and they trust that parents mean what they say.
- **Family Bonding**: Regular activities together, such as playing board games or cooking, create memories and closeness. This shared time can reduce sibling fights and build a sense of unity.

When children learn that their family is a safe place to express fears, anger, or sadness, they develop healthier ways to solve conflicts outside the home, too.

Balancing Independence and Guidance

As children grow older, they crave more independence. Parents can support this by letting them make choices, like which club to join or how to decorate their bedroom, while still setting boundaries around respect. If a parent micromanages every decision, the child might feel resentful, sometimes acting out by bullying at school. If they are given too much freedom without guidance, they might not learn to handle relationships responsibly. A balance—showing trust in the child but guiding them when needed—helps them form positive bonds with peers and adults.

Encouraging Empathy in Friendships

Outside the home, friendships are a major part of a child's life. Encouraging empathy within these friendships can prevent bullying:

- **Group Discussions**: Teachers or after-school leaders can hold quick talks about what makes a good friend. Answers might include listening, sharing, and offering help.
- **Conflict Resolution**: When friends argue, an adult can guide them to use words like "I feel…" and "I need…" instead of shouting. Over time, they pick up habits of respectful problem-solving.
- **Inclusion**: Reminding children to look out for classmates who seem lonely or new can help them form inclusive friendships rather than exclusive cliques.

Empathy-focused friendships often create a social network that rejects bullying. Children do not want to harm someone they genuinely care about, and they step in if a friend is bullied.

Team-Building in Classrooms

Teachers can support positive relationships by using group tasks that require cooperation rather than competition. For example, science projects can be done in teams where each student has a role. If a class is divided into smaller groups to complete a shared goal, students learn to depend on each other's strengths. They see that each member—no matter how quiet or different—brings something useful. This appreciation of differences can lower the risk of teasing or exclusion.

In addition, classroom rules might include statements like "We support one another's efforts," "We use kind words," and "We celebrate each other's successes." Although children may not always live up to these ideals, the repeated reminders help set a caring tone.

Peer Support Groups

Another way to foster positive relationships is to form peer support groups, where students meet regularly to share concerns or give each other advice. A teacher or counselor might lead these groups at first, then gradually let students take more responsibility. By talking openly about stress, worries, and achievements, participants learn they are not alone. This lowers the tension that can lead to bullying. They also build friendships across different social circles, breaking down the cliques that often fuel bullying.

Encouraging Acts of Kindness

Schools and families can highlight small acts of kindness, such as helping a classmate pick up spilled books, inviting a lonely student to join a game, or sending a supportive note to someone who seems stressed. These acts do not have to be big or fancy, but they can build connection and trust. Some classrooms have a kindness board where students can write down nice things they observed their classmates doing. This keeps everyone thinking about how to be considerate and can inspire others to do the same.

Respect for Differences

Often, bullying targets people who are different in some way—because of their appearance, background, interests, or abilities. Supporting positive relationships means teaching respect for differences. This can include:

- **Sharing Cultures**: Allowing children to talk about their family traditions or favorite foods, letting classmates appreciate variety.
- **Guest Speakers**: Inviting visitors who can talk about life with a disability or about life in a different country can open eyes to new perspectives.
- **Literature and Media**: Reading stories or watching short videos that show diverse characters in a positive light. This helps children see the value in being unique.

When children learn that differences are not threats but interesting parts of who we are, they are less likely to mock someone who stands out.

Guiding Group Activities

Sports teams, school bands, drama clubs, and other group activities can build positive relationships when they are led with care. Coaches and leaders can set the expectation that everyone supports each other. If a star player insults a less skilled teammate, the coach should address it quickly, reminding them that the team thrives on respect. When a band member laughs at another's mistake, the leader can model how to encourage or give constructive feedback instead. By keeping the focus on shared goals and growth, these activities become environments where bullying does not fit.

Teacher-Student Connections

A caring teacher-student relationship can be a major protective factor. If students trust their teacher, they feel safer reporting bullying. They also have a role model who shows them how to handle anger or disagreements calmly. Teachers can build these connections by:

- **Greeting Students Individually**: A simple smile or friendly word at the start of class can make a child feel noticed.
- **Asking About Interests**: Teachers who remember a student's hobby—like drawing, soccer, or animals—show that they see them as individuals.
- **Checking In**: If a student looks upset, a teacher might ask quietly if they need to talk.
- **Being Consistent**: Following through on promises and treating all students fairly builds trust.

Children who feel connected to a teacher often respect classroom rules more, including anti-bullying expectations.

Mentoring Roles for Students

We sometimes think only adults can be mentors, but older students can guide younger ones. This approach benefits both sides. Younger students gain a friendly helper they can look up to. Older students learn responsibility and empathy. Typical ways to set this up:

- **Reading Buddies**: A fifth grader reads with a first grader once a week. They share books and talk about stories, building a caring bond.
- **Schoolwide Mentoring**: Middle schoolers might mentor elementary students, leading games or helping with homework.

- **Peer Tutors**: High-achieving students help those who struggle academically, forming respectful relationships instead of teasing.

This culture of older students caring for younger ones sends a strong message: we look out for each other here.

Helping Children Navigate Social Media

In today's world, digital relationships are just as real as face-to-face ones. Parents, teachers, and mentors can support positive online relationships by teaching:

- **Respectful Posting**: Remind children that everything they post can affect others' feelings. Jokes should never be cruel or threatening.
- **Responsible Sharing**: Encourage them to ask permission before sharing photos or personal details about friends.
- **Mindful Replying**: Pause before sending an angry message. If upset, wait and calm down first.
- **Seeing Each Other as People**: Even though it is just a screen, they should remember there is a real person behind each username.

Building respectful online habits is vital to preventing cyberbullying and maintaining positive friendships in digital spaces.

Conflict as a Chance to Grow

Even in the best relationships, conflicts happen. Children do not need to avoid all disagreements. In fact, seeing conflict as a normal part of life can lower the panic that leads to bullying. Adults can show children that conflicts can be handled without hurting each other:

- **Listening to Understand**: Each side shares what is bothering them, while the other side listens quietly.
- **Looking for Mutual Solutions**: They ask, "How can we fix this so both of us feel okay?"
- **Avoiding Blame**: Instead of saying "It's your fault," they focus on "I feel..." or "I need..."
- **Forgiveness and Moving On**: If someone truly apologizes and makes amends, let the conflict pass rather than holding grudges.

When children learn to handle conflicts peacefully, they realize they do not have to use mean words or threats to solve problems.

Personal Growth Activities

Building positive relationships also means helping children grow as individuals. If a child feels secure in their skills and identity, they are less likely to become a bully or a target. Activities that promote self-growth:

- **Self-Reflection**: Encouraging journaling, where children can write about their day, their feelings, and any conflicts they faced.
- **Goal-Setting**: Letting children set small personal goals, like learning a new skill or being kind to someone each day. Achieving these goals builds confidence.
- **Mindfulness**: Simple breathing exercises or quiet moments can help them manage stress or anger, reducing harsh behavior toward others.
- **Positive Feedback**: Pointing out their strengths, such as creativity or teamwork, helps them appreciate themselves without stepping on others to feel important.

Family Nights and Community Events

Positive relationships can grow when families and neighbors come together. Events such as a school open house, sports day, or a community picnic give children the chance to see each other in a relaxed setting outside of class. They might realize they share interests with peers they barely knew. Parents might get to know each other too, forming a supportive network. When communities are connected, bullying has less space to flourish.

Rewarding Cooperation and Kindness

Some schools or families create simple reward systems for cooperation. This does not have to be material (like giving out candy) but can be recognition:

- **"Kindness Shout-Outs"**: A teacher publicly thanks a student who helped a classmate.
- **Team Points**: A group of students earn a point each time they show teamwork, aiming for a small class treat.
- **Certificates**: Handing out a simple paper certificate acknowledging a child's respectful behavior or helpful actions.

Such rewards highlight the value of empathy. They also show that positive relationships matter to the whole group.

Bystander Empowerment

We covered bystanders in the previous chapter, but supporting bystanders is also part of building positive relationships. When children realize they do not have to go against a bully alone, but can rely on friends, the power of bullying fades. Encouraging children to check on someone who is targeted, or to stand with a friend who speaks up, strengthens those peer bonds. This sense of unity keeps bullies from isolating their targets.

Modeling from Adults
Above all, adults must model the behavior they want to see. If teachers gossip about one student to another, or if a parent yells insults during a sports game, children notice. They might think, "If grown-ups act like that, it must be okay for me to do it too." On the other hand, if children see adults handle frustration politely, apologize when they make mistakes, and treat people with fairness, they learn that this is the normal, right way to behave. Modeling is one of the strongest teaching tools because children often copy what they see.

Lasting Impact of Positive Relationships
Children who experience supportive bonds early in life carry those lessons into adulthood. They learn to value teamwork, to show empathy, and to approach disagreements with calm rather than hostility. This can shape the culture of schools and workplaces for years to come. As these children grow, they might become mentors themselves, passing on the kindness they experienced. In a broader sense, strong relationships protect against not just bullying but many social problems, because respect and care are at the heart of any healthy community.

Moving Ahead with Hope
Through this book, we have looked deeply into what bullying is, why it happens, how it affects everyone involved, and how it can be stopped. We have talked about the social and emotional factors, family influences, school policies, community support, and restorative methods that can bring real change. Now, as we conclude, remember that all these solutions work best when they rest on a foundation of positive relationships. Children thrive when they sense that people care about them and want them to do well, both at home and at school. Bullying fades when children see one another not as enemies but as classmates, neighbors, or friends who share the same environment.

No plan is perfect. There will always be challenges and moments of conflict. But when we focus on building and maintaining strong bonds, we create resilience. Children learn they can rely on each other and on caring adults. They learn that hurting someone else does not solve problems, and that asking for help is not a weakness. They begin to understand that kindness is not just a rule—it is the best way for all of us to live and learn together.

So, whether you are a parent, teacher, counselor, friend, or student, you have the power to support positive relationships in your circle. Listen with patience. Stand up if you see someone being mistreated. Offer a smile or a helping hand to someone who is alone. Step in calmly if conflicts arise and encourage solutions that respect everyone. These small, everyday choices shape a safer, healthier environment where bullying cannot easily grow. By championing kindness, understanding, and support, we ensure that children grow up with the emotional tools they need—turning the tide against bullying and making respect the guiding principle in every interaction.

www.ingramcontent.com/pod-product-compliance
Lightning Source LLC
LaVergne TN
LVHW012108070526
838202LV00056B/5668